THE
BIG
RISK

NAVIGATE THE LAND MINES
OF SUDDEN WEALTH

WALTER CLARKE

ISBN (hardcover): 979-8-9878019-5-6

CONTENTS

INTRODUCTION

There are a lot of books on how to get rich. This isn't one of them.

It is about what to do when you're suddenly rich, so you don't screw it up.

It is about how to manage that type of wealth, so it doesn't manage *you*.

It is about how to understand the concept of risk — risk as it relates to wealth — so that your wealth will flourish, not fail.

When you attain sudden wealth, you experience new risks that didn't previously exist in your life. This is a book about understanding and preventing, or at least minimizing, those risks. Some of these are investment strategies; others are more psychological in nature, diving deeper into why you may or may not make certain choices or follow a path peppered with risk.

The truth is, you don't know what you don't know and that complexity of limited understanding breeds risk. As someone who came face to face with what they didn't know head-on — and has since helped the suddenly wealthy become suddenly wise — I'm here to walk you through this.

Think about it: In so many things in life, we prepare for the worst-case scenario. We buy health insurance in case of a medical emergency and auto insurance for a possible accident. Business owners create contracts to protect themselves and their business. Some people draft prenups to safeguard their assets heading into a marriage. People do all of this to mitigate their risk.

It may sound negative, but preparing for the worst-case scenario is quite the opposite; it's putting your best interests at the forefront. Hoping you won't land in the ER or lose all your wealth in a risky move is not enough. It's not smart practice to lead a life hinging on hope. You need to prepare for prosperity by thinking ahead. This is how you win the game.

So, then what about the risks under a guise of something the complete opposite — risks masked as a gift, like money? Those who come into an influx of wealth can be so blindsided by the allure of a padded bank account that they neglect how to nurture their assets.

But why? Why do people so easily mismanage their sudden wealth? It's because they misunderstand their newly inherited risk and they get arrogant, even negligent, about risks. People who quickly come into a lot of wealth — whether from selling a successful business, receiving an inheritance, or being awarded a large settlement — rarely understand how to actually manage it.

And wealth, poorly handled, can actually make life much worse. You could lose your house, experience familial distress, or have to sell treasured heirlooms. You don't want to be forced into merely staying afloat. Rather, you want your wealth to keep you flying high.

I want you to take that sudden wealth and build *sustainable* wealth over a long period, a lifetime. You do this by avoiding the financial traps that follow a windfall of wealth and by remaining humble. Humility is vital. When you are humble, you proceed with a level of caution that keeps you out of trouble.

And don't worry about maximizing every dollar. Avoid the traps and even mediocre investment returns will result in a lifetime of financial security.

You might be thinking, "This advice is for amateurs," but the managers of Silicon Valley Bank (SVB) would fervently disagree. Like many newly rich, SVB experienced explosive growth (i.e., sudden wealth), with its status as the preferred bank of Silicon Valley leading to a surge in bank deposits (at one time, SVB had over $500 billion in assets). And, like many newly rich, the managers of SVB didn't understand what to do with this level of quick growth. Parking the bank's funds in U.S. government treasuries to take advantage of the Fed's low interest rate policy seemed like an easy and safe way to maximize returns.

However, this was a massive risk. SVB fell into a financial trap, putting all of their assets in one place and making a one-way bet that could only get worse as the Fed began to raise interest rates. If SVB were ever forced to sell these assets, it would likely take large losses, and the significant amount of non-FDIC insured deposits made a forced sale plausible.

How big were these losses? On March 8, 2023, each share of SVB stock was worth $267.83. By the end of the month, that stock price had plummeted to 40 cents. SVB lost over 99.8% of its value practically overnight, leaving shareholders shocked as their wealth had evaporated.

If SVB had measured risk differently, returns may have been lower but the bank would have survived. Managers would still have their jobs and shareholders would still have their money.

The string of events that led to the collapse of SVB in March 2023 is something I have witnessed, and experienced, first-hand. People can be just fine during the calm, but when the crisis inevitably arrives, it can be catastrophic. Just as swiftly as they got their sudden wealth, it is not safe and their financial future is at risk. Even extremely intelligent people can find themselves in this situation, failing to understand the risks they face. People think they are smart (and maybe they are) but they don't know what they don't know. None of us do. The reality is: The chance of loss is always lurking around the corner, no matter who you are or what you do. And if you're not ready for the crisis, the crisis will take you down.

I have spent the last decade educating others on sudden wealth. The prevalent pattern I've seen is this: People make obvious mistakes because they get arrogant and think they know what's going to happen, then their returns usually suffer (or worse). Whereas, those that remain humble, understand risks, and target reasonable returns do significantly better.

In this book, I will take you on an odyssey of tripwires you don't know exist, with a goal of empowering you to manage your wealth with less fallibility and more foresight. I want to teach you to look at both sides of the coin—all that you can do with your wealth and all that it can do to you. In other words, all of the possibilities with your wealth and all of the problems. This is how you structure a life where your money does not manage you.

You, and you alone, are the master of your money. And your money can either limit your life or expand it. Sudden wealth isn't built to last without the right tools, mindset, and understanding of what could be around the corner. Let's make it last.

CHAPTER 1
THE CONNECTION BETWEEN EXCESSIVE OPTIMISM AND UNEXPECTED RISK

"It takes 20 years to build a reputation and five minutes to ruin it. If you think about that, you'll do things differently."

– *Warren Buffett*

I was visiting a TD Ameritrade office in Denver — the day was May 20, 2012 — when I got the phone call from my securities attorney that changed my life. And not in a good way.

"Sit down," he said.

He'd just been on the phone with the Securities and Exchange Commission (SEC). They had informed him that they had just launched an administrative proceeding against me before the SEC. It would be on their website within the next couple of hours. A press release to local and national media would follow.

Hell of a phone call.

The course of my career, and life, would be forever changed.

Nearly 10 years earlier, I had launched Oxford Investment Partners. At the time, I was wary of the traditional commission-based structure that's so common among financial and investment advisers. I felt it was inherently rigged. There had to be another way, and I was determined to find it.

Oxford debuted in 2003 with eight clients and $50 million in assets. We had an attractive business model that allowed high-net-worth families to invest in a variety of alternative investment vehicles, mostly focused on real estate, and it brought quick success. By the end of 2007, we had grown to $350 million in assets and just under $3 million in annual revenue.

Our growth was quick and the money that followed was sudden, so there were plenty of reasons to celebrate. And I did. As my business took off, I got caught up in what I can only call a kind of business euphoria. I decided I could do no wrong and that my business success would continue, that thriving was par for the course.

Given that eventual phone call, it's clear I was a bit overly optimistic.

At the time, however, you couldn't have convinced me anything would derail my career. As my wealth grew, so did my arrogance.

Since the firm was so wildly successful, in 2007 my wife and I decided to buy a new house that was still under construction.

The house was expensive, but hey, the business was going so well that I justified the huge mortgage quite easily, knowing that a bank would approve it. After all, I had a seven-figure income.

I was right about one thing: We got approved for the mortgage (like just about everyone with a pulse during the real estate boom in 2007). So, we bought the new house and put our old one on the market. And like every other construction project during this time, construction costs ballooned — to three times what I had expected.

I was making $125,000 a month, and yet, I had NO MONEY. This alone was a wakeup call, but then the housing market began to slow down. I reviewed my balance sheet and realized I had far too much mortgage debt. I knew I needed to unload some of my liabilities. But I'd already sold the other house. At that point, I only had one asset I could sell: my business.

I offered a portion of it to three people:

- My largest and most important client.
- An outside professional investor who was friends with that large client.
- My mother.

Given that my business was very complex, I hired a team of lawyers to make sure the transactions were structured properly. This was completed in 2008 and included selling 15% of the firm to the three parties under the assumption that everything we did was perfectly legal.

As luck would have it, three months after the sale was finalized, the SEC came by to do a routine examination. It was the first time Oxford had been examined by the SEC in its five-year history. I was nervous but also curious to see what the examiners would say about the sale.

And when the SEC didn't call out the sale as problematic, I breathed a huge sigh of relief. We'd indeed gotten it right. I felt like I could rest a little easier knowing the examination was over and we could move on with our lives.

But, my celebration turned out to be short-lived.

Because Oxford was heavily involved in real estate, the SEC returned to our office in 2009. It began a second examination to make sure our clients held the type of real estate interests we claimed they did.

Examination number two was <u>VERY</u> different than examination number one.

From the onset, the whole tone was dissimilar. Instead of staying one week, the examiners stayed for one month. They constantly asked for additional documents, and not just about one or two properties, but for *every one* of our real estate projects.

This time, they were particularly curious about the transaction in which I sold a portion of my firm. I explained that the last examination covered the sale and no issues were found, not that the new examiners cared about that.

They just kept digging … and digging.

Throughout the examination, I had a nagging feeling I couldn't quite put my finger on.

But about 18 months after the second examination began, when I got that phone call, things became all too clear.

On the call, I learned the SEC would be issuing a Wells Notice, alleging I had violated securities law, including exploiting an Oxford client by artificially inflating the value of my firm by at least $1.5 million which, in turn, raised the sale price of those ownership stakes.[1]

To say I was shocked is an understatement. Remember, I didn't have any complaints from clients, and the first examination didn't reveal any issues. And to my understanding, I had done everything right. I later learned a tough lesson: Just because you think you're doing something right doesn't necessarily mean that you are. You don't know what you don't know, and that can lead you down an unintended wrong path.

To save my reputation and business — I was also a respected instructor at several universities at the time — I considered taking the whole matter to court. I was self-righteous and angry. But I didn't.

Looking back, I see that mistakes were made. At the heart of the issue is something called a principal transaction, which my business had never done before (we usually did agency transactions) and requires a different set of disclosure requirements. The rules around this are clear, but we didn't understand them. Therefore, my team didn't execute the transaction correctly. And more importantly, the SEC doesn't like it when an adviser sells his own assets to a client without the extra care and disclosure required to protect the client.

I had strayed from the business practices I knew and paid the ultimate price. I learned the hard way that one bad mistake in business has far greater consequences than a long history of good decisions.

So, I settled the case. I was banned from securities trading for two years, paid over $274,000 in fines, and I lost my $10 million business.

And you know what? The SEC was right. I should have known better, but my lifestyle pressures — which I had freely chosen — clouded my judgment. The investigators from the SEC are not the bad guys here.

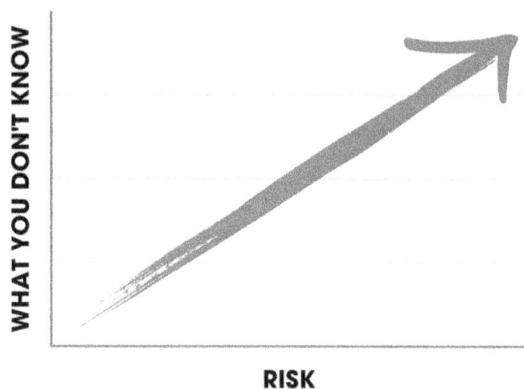

I'm NOT going to claim that I was a victim. The truth is, we overspent and then went into debt. And because I was in debt, I made bad decisions.

When you're in debt, you're compromised. When you're compromised, you make poor choices. It's like going to the supermarket when you haven't eaten all day. You're likely to spend more because everything looks so good and you're hungry.

I was also being overly optimistic about my future income. I only focused on the short-term and completely ignored the long-term effect of my spending decisions.

I call this the spending trap.

Wealth is measured by how much cash flow is left after all your bills and expenses are paid. *It is not calculated by how much stuff you have!*

Wealth is created by not falling into this trap. I came to these conclusions by losing nearly everything I had ever treasured.

Following my SEC ban, I was forced to sell my business. I became a pariah in my community. My marriage didn't survive. There went the dream home. And, worst of all, my children were disappointed in me.

But eventually there was an unexpected silver lining in this mess.

Before the SEC ban, I was on a hamster wheel working to maintain a "never enough" lifestyle of private schools, fancy cars, big homes, and luxurious vacations. The FX series "Fleishman is in Trouble," based on a novel by Taffy Brodesser-Akner, is covering some of this ground as I write.[2]

There was no way I'd have been able to step off that wheel by myself. The SEC's ruling was, in effect, a forced reboot. A mandated time-out. And with that downtime came a surprising sense of relief.

I began to assess the impact of the choices, big and small, that I'd made. I developed the wherewithal (I certainly had newfound time) to reflect on how I'd gotten to where I was.

My life is now divided into two phases: pre-SEC ban and post-SEC ban. In the pre-ban world, I traveled for business and basically never left the hotel. Post-ban, I don't travel without my bike. Before the ban, I swept in and out of cities and hurried home without taking in the sights. After the ban, I add a day to my trips to explore whatever city I'm visiting.

After the dust settled, one particular moment was a turning point.

I was in San Francisco for a meeting. I mentioned to a colleague that I had my bicycle with me. Someone at the meeting invited me to a group ride the following morning.

The old me would never have considered this, but the new me wouldn't miss it.

So, a little after 7:00 a.m., we were riding across the Golden Gate Bridge. I'd grown up in the Bay Area but had never ridden across its most famous bridge — heck, one of the most famous structures in the world. That day, I did it twice.

Have you ever had that feeling that something is missing in your life? And you think that if you run faster, you'll catch it?

I'd been chasing that missing piece, trying to fill that void, for years. But on that early, crisp morning in San Francisco, I found peace. At last, I was where I needed to be.

For the first time, I began to thank the SEC for burning my life to the ground. It allowed me to build it back up again.

And from all those hard lessons, painful nights, and tears comes this book.

THE ULTRA-RICH PLAN

This book will teach you how the ultra-rich control their spending and build their wealth over time (and you don't have to start out rich to go the ultra-rich route). I'll give you examples of how to view saving and investing and showcase decisions that smart money managers make every day.

My concept breaks down into two simple ways of viewing money:

1. You as the earner.
2. Your investments as the earner.

The ultra-rich understand the importance of controlling spending, setting aside excuses for not investing, and getting money to grow.

They understand the negative effects of debt. They understand that free cash flow is the measure of success.

The ultra-poor, no matter their income, measure success by how much stuff they own.

They are forever slaves to their lifestyle. Take it from someone who had it all, and lost it, this is no way to live.

Because I know what it feels like to start from scratch, I've made it my mission to stop people from making the kind of financial mistakes I made. What you don't know will hurt you. My mission has allowed me to see what I once considered the lowest moment of my life with clarity and turn it into something of value.

It is my goal to simplify needlessly complicated financial processes and make them accessible to everyone.

At the end of the day, it's your money. No one will look after it like you will. The goal is to put you back in the driver's seat, to empower you to steer the course you want.

LESSONS AT A GLANCE

- Understand what you're doing, especially when you put your wealth at risk.
- When things are going great, don't assume that's the norm.
- Don't fall into the spending trap.
- Get off the hamster wheel.

CHAPTER 2
THE EFFECT OF
SUDDEN WEALTH

"It's not how much money you make, but how much money you keep, how hard it works for you, and how many generations you keep it for. "

– Robert Kiyosaki

Sometimes, people hit it big. They wake up rich, where it literally happens overnight. While it has been referred to as the Cinderella complex, many call this phenomenon sudden wealth.

Quite simply, it can be defined in two ways:

1. Gaining a life-changing increase in income.
2. A large sum of money becomes immediately available.

Consider some scenarios:

- A young artist's new single takes off, and she's rewarded with a lucrative recording contract.
- A high school sports prodigy inks a pro deal, and he gets a big signing bonus.
- A social media star becomes the face of a global lifestyle brand, and royalty checks start pouring in.
- A successful family business is sold and family members receive $50 million each.
- A couple gets divorced and a large settlement is awarded to one of the spouses.
- Children or grandchildren inherit a large sum after a death in the family.

The startup multimillionaire or billionaire is a relatively new occurrence and certainly a sign of the times. As tech companies go public or garner massive valuations, there are entire swaths of Silicon Valley engineers and product managers who have found themselves catapulted into previously unattainable tax brackets within a matter of hours.

This has happened before. In the 1990s when the internet was commercialized, the dot-com boom took off. During the 19th-century, the oil and railroad booms gave us the Gilded Age.

WHAT MAKES SUDDEN WEALTH DIFFERENT

Typically, people become millionaires in three ways. Either they are born into wealth, they grow their wealth over time, or they come into their wealth through a sudden windfall. To illustrate the effect of sudden wealth, I'll focus on the latter two.

Those who grow their wealth over time are the "millionaires next door." They are savers whose fiscal discipline is firmly in place. They are frugal, often buying things they want or need when on sale. They drive standard domestic cars instead of bespoke fancy foreign sports cars (and they don't lease). They don't take on debt that won't eventually increase their net worth. They are patient and calculated with their money and have refined a specific skill set over the years to create wealth. They are also very likely to keep their money once they earn it.

Sudden wealth, on the other hand, is the complete opposite. As I mentioned before, it represents a drastic change in fiscal circumstances. Let LeBron James explain it:

> Being a first-generational money-maker in the household is a scary thing for an 18-year-old. I went from sitting in classrooms and, in May, graduating high school, to being a multimillionaire a month later, in June, which is insane.[1]

Sudden wealth is not earned gradually through a series of extremely frugal choices or wise investments. People who come into sudden wealth aren't likely to have had the financial or internal discipline required to grow *some* money into *a lot* of money — which means they're far more likely to mismanage it (though LeBron did just fine, as I'll explain later).

What makes these two subsets of people so different? It mainly comes down to behavior, habits, and mindset.

People often use money as a way to make themselves appear better, or at least in a way that makes them perceive themselves as better.

They come to see possessions as the external proof of their happiness and their self-worth and feel entitled to live lavishly. They have the money, therefore they should live large. And it helps them keep up the appearance that they're happy.

Millionaires next door aren't doing this. They're not using the money to purchase *things* to make themselves feel better or broadcast the illusion that they're happy. They're using money as a utilitarian tool to grow their net worth.

TWO WAYS OF VIEWING SUDDEN WEALTH

1. What can my money buy?

When some people come into sudden wealth, they immediately begin to think about all the *things* they can buy now that they're millionaires or billionaires. Individuals with this mindset fall perfectly into the spending trap.

It's easy to get caught up in this mentality — and money can be spent much faster than people realize. Messages to buy new things are inescapable. Marketing, an inescapable part of contemporary American culture, has effectively managed to equate material goods with validation, success, and happiness.

Even motivational speakers tell you to visualize the things you want in order to inspire you to work harder. Picture that massive house, see that dream vacation, feel the driver's seat in that fancy new car. But what they're doing is essentially encouraging you to earn money so you can spend every last cent of it.

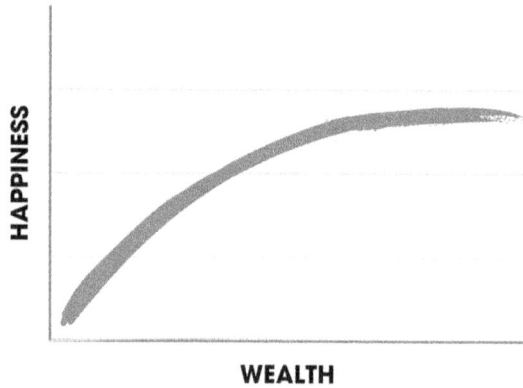

That's a pretty terrible trade. While this might be considered motivational for some, it isn't necessarily sound financial advice.

And let's face it, $10 million can buy you a lot of *stuff*. Maybe you and your spouse go on a shopping spree and buy a bigger house, trade in the old cars, and hell, splurge on that boat you've always wanted, even if you don't know how to drive one. (But it's OK because now you can afford lessons and can ignore the fact that a boat will literally sink your money.)

The desire to spend is an understandable reaction, but it's also an emotional one, especially if you've never had much money before.

Even rational, intelligent people can be driven to make less-than-rational decisions when they suddenly find themselves in a position of wealth.

People who view money this way — as a means to buy more for themselves and appear successful — are looking for external validation, as opposed to seeing wealth as a tool.

THE BIG RISK   15

But no matter how many things you buy, they will never make you feel as good as you hoped they would.

Of course, this leads to buying something bigger, more expensive, or more coveted, with the same result every time. Eventually you become disillusioned, dissatisfied, and disappointed. The majority of the time, people who view sudden wealth this way end up losing their wealth.

FALLING INTO THE TRAP

With these very common human tendencies in mind, let's consider the problem of sudden money. As rapper Biggie Smalls (aka Notorious B.I.G.) so appropriately proclaimed in the late '90s: "Mo' money, mo' problems."[2] And it's true — tragic stories of lottery winners abound, including many tales of wild spending, mismanagement, and crime.[3]

In fact, lottery winners go broke so often, there's a so-called "lottery curse."[4]

Researchers in a 2010 study found that a comparison of Florida jackpot winners who received between $50,000 and $150,000 only *postponed* bankruptcy if they were already in danger of it. And winners of large jackpots that later filed for bankruptcy ended up with similar net assets and unsecured debt as small winners.[5]

Many years ago, one of my colleagues advised a bright young artist who hit it big. The singer met with my friend to discuss his new wealth and how he planned to spend it. The family would no longer fly commercial, he said. He was going to buy a big RV for touring, along with a new house and some cars. He said he could afford it all.

His financial adviser, however, knew these expenses would eat up his money. Additionally, most artists get hot … and then not.

There's never a guarantee that another hit song, new contract, or sold-out tour is actually going to happen down the road.

So, he sat the singer down and told him, "We're going to freeze spending at your current levels. Your new windfall is going into an asset bucket. We're going to create freedom."

This conversation can be hard to have with any client, let alone a celebrity.

What the financial adviser knew is that many celebrities are famous, but not rich. He wanted his client to be both rich *and* famous, even in the (likely) event that his career went cold. Because he made a short-term sacrifice, that artist now has long-term stability.

But it certainly could have gone the other way.

There's probably no other artist more associated with poor money choices than hip-hop star MC Hammer, who rose to fame in the late '80s.

According to *Forbes*, MC Hammer (born Stanley Kirk Burrell) was worth $33 million at his peak in 1991. But within five years, it was all gone.

In 2014, Thrillist published an article detailing how the hip-hop star had spent his fortune.[6] According to the report, Hammer bankrolled a 200-person payroll that ran him at least $500,000 a month and built a $30 million mansion that included a 33-person theater, a baseball diamond, multiple tennis courts, and a stable that housed 19 thoroughbred racing horses.

By 1996, the entire fortune had been depleted. And not only was the money gone, but he was $13 million in debt due to burning through his money at about $6.6 million per year ($550,000 per month) — a staggeringly high 18% distribution rate. Since his payroll alone cost him nearly that whole amount, it's not hard to see how he ended up in debt.

Even though he was "worth" $33 million, Hammer was poor. To get himself back on a solid footing, he sold his house for a fraction of what he spent building it. After that, he became a minister, and more recently, a startup consultant.

To be fair to Hammer, he's not the only star to dramatically mismanage his money or spend himself out of his extravagant lifestyle.

Country legend Willie Nelson also made headlines in the '90s for owing the IRS over $10 million. Things were so bleak that he had his guitar, "Trigger," exiled out of Texas, just in case the IRS tried to seize it and auction it off for taxes due.[7]

In 2011, the IRS sued rapper Nas for over $6.4 million in back taxes. That same year, he was also reportedly struggling to pay his mortgage, child support, and alimony.[8]

In 2013, Grammy winner Lauryn Hill served a prison term for tax evasion.[9] In 2014, mega-producer Jermaine Dupri lost his $3.7 million Atlanta mansion for failing to keep up with his mortgage payments.[10]

Actor Johnny Depp managed to blow through his multimillion-dollar fortune, and although he blamed it on his financial advisers — prompting a $25 million lawsuit alleging fraud and negligence in 2017 — they cited his ultra-lavish lifestyle as the reason for his money troubles.[11]

According to multiple sources, Depp's expenses ballooned to $2 million *per month* at one point, not including that time he paid $3 million (some sources say $5 million) to shoot Hunter S. Thompson's ashes out of a custom-made cannon over the city of Aspen, Colorado.

Actor, singer, and omnipresent '70s heartthrob David Cassidy filed for bankruptcy a few years before his death in 2017, citing assets and debt totaling $10 million to various parties. He reportedly was only able to leave about $150,000 in assets to his son.[12]

You get the picture.

HOW THE HELL DOES THIS HAPPEN?

The key question from all of these examples is how this happens. Why would anyone making millions a year take on any debt at all?

All of the above money problems were entirely, and wholly, avoidable. That's the real tragedy. Everyone with wealth has the power to make the right choices. The main problem is that most people have no idea what their burn rate is — in other words, how quickly they go through money.

Questions to ask yourself:

1. Do you know how much you spent last month on, say, eating out at restaurants?
2. Do you know how much you spent on holiday gifts last year?

Many people have no idea. They cannot answer these simple questions. A further complication is the effect financial pressure has on people, which often leads to poor decision-making.

Peer pressure is another factor. It's common for people to let their judgment be clouded by where they *think* they should be in their lives, as opposed to where they actually are, and this happens at every income level, in every industry. We see people living the way they *wish* they could live or taking vacations they've always *wanted* to take. A few years ago, I spoke with a Hollywood celebrity who was spending $100,000 on weekend trips abroad because that's "just what people did."

So many of us overextend ourselves to reach for something that seems affordable at the time, but given the right economic downturn or unexpected circumstance, puts us at risk.

Keep in mind: Just because you QUALIFY for it, doesn't mean you can AFFORD it.

In my experience, more people make this mistake than don't. Furthermore, there's a relationship between spending and assets that most people don't understand, especially the broader variability in the case of high-income earners.

If you earn an average of $50,000 per year, that amount will most likely only vary maybe $10,000 in either direction. But with high-income earners, it's a much longer pendulum that can swing to greater extremes.

If you average $2 million per year, you could end up with $5 million one year and $1 million the year after that. And if you spend like you're going to earn $5 million every year, you're going to end up in the red a hell of a lot faster than you realize.

Musical artists are a great example of this because they earn the bulk of their money when they're touring. Paul McCartney earned $132 million[13] during his 2017 "One on One" tour, but in a non-touring year, he might only earn $2 million. But if he spent like he was going to earn $132 million next year, and the next, and the next, he'd end up like Hammer.

What the high-income earner needs to recognize is that his or her income can (and will) go down during economic cycles. The greater your income, the greater its degree of variability.

By 2009, my personal income dropped 50% practically overnight. I didn't think that was possible. But I saw it with my own eyes during a perfect storm of events. It's *imperative* to plan for the inevitable times when income drops dramatically. It's not a matter of *if* it will happen, but *when*.

2. What can my money support?

People who grow (or at the very least, keep) their fortune aren't focused on the *things* they can buy. Instead, they're focused on what their money can *support*. In order to understand what money can support, a completely different mindset must be embraced.

These people understand that having a pile of money doesn't make you rich. They understand that it's more about how you spend it, and that there's a relationship between spending and assets.

The lavish lifestyle most people think they can embrace after coming into sudden wealth — with the cars and the mansions and the dream vacations — won't last as long as they think it will.

It can't last because that kind of lifestyle can't be supported in perpetuity. *When* the downturn happens, you'll be going backward fast.

On the opposite end of the spectrum, if you're viewing wealth as a tool, you do things a bit differently.

If you're assuming a 4% distribution rate (widely considered sustainable), which amounts to living on $400,000 per year (assuming $240,000 after taxes), $10 million can support you for 25 years.

But if you were to take that $10 million and spend it at a rapid rate, you might be left with only $5 million. Living on $400,000 a year, you've now cut the life of your sudden wealth in half. You've depleted the principal, and you're on your way to being poor.

Let's say Hammer spent $2 million each year on his lifestyle (and taxes) and invested $16 million. After three years, that $16 million would've turned into $48 million (and then basically be guaranteed, if invested wisely, to generate returns forever). He could've lived on $1.9 million per year for the next 25 years based on just three years of being "frugal."

A short-term sacrifice, and a series of wise investments, could have turned into a lifetime of stability.

Another strategy would have been to take the typical 4% distribution rate and live off $1.3 million per year, which would have lasted until he was at least 54 years old. This would have provided the funds for passion projects, which might have enabled him to create new revenue streams that built additional wealth.

Having passive income like this frees up your time so you can focus on things you actually *want* to do, instead of engaging in the rat race of needing earned income to survive. You could start a new business venture and create your dream job. You could make calculated investments in new businesses and obtain new wealth. Or you could just go to the beach.

The world could be your oyster.

Examples of wealthy people who've managed their money well aren't as easy to come by. Oftentimes it's not smart, sensible people who end up trending on Twitter. It's the MC Hammers and the Johnny Depps of the world who are in the headlines for making insane amounts of money and somehow ending up in bankruptcy.

But success stories are out there too, and they're just as important to consider.

Dolly Parton, for example, is getting as famous for her philanthropy as her singing and songwriting.[14] But she wouldn't have so much money to give away if she hadn't been so savvy with it.

This included setting up her own music publishing company when she was only 20 years old (no easy feat for a woman in the dog-eat-dog music business of the mid-1960s). It has been a veritable printing press of money ever since. No one else gets a cut of the royalty streams from all those great songs she wrote, like Whitney Houston's megahit cover of "I Will Always Love You," the royalties from which Parton invested in an African-American neighborhood in Nashville.[15] According to *Forbes*, Parton's songbook brings in $6 to $8 million annually and is worth a cool $150 million.[16]

Among other things, with this revenue stream she developed Dollywood (of which she owns a 50% stake). It's ranked as one of the best amusement parks in the world and valued at upward of $150 million.

The bottom line is that you need to take the structure of a stable business operation and incorporate it into your personal life.

Much like with a business, replenishing the money you're spending has to remain a priority. You need to figure out how fast you can match your earned income to your passive income so you can have free cash flow.

Let's go back to Hammer one more time. Remember that he was spending around $6.6 million per year and was worth $33 million. In order to sustain that level of spending — and to make sure the pot was being replenished at a responsible rate — he needed to be earning $132 million every single year. He'd need to be touring Paul McCartney's 37-show tour, at $145 per ticket, on a nonstop basis.

There aren't many acts that can draw that kind of crowd at that price point — and definitely not forever.

ARE YOU RICH OR ARE YOU POOR?

At the end of the day, which of these behaviors and attitudes best describe you? Are you focused on what sudden wealth can *buy* you or how it can *support* you?

Do you know what your burn rate is? Do you have free cash flow?

How do you even know if you're overextending yourself?

It's actually quite easy to measure. It's all about what's coming in versus what's going out.

Let's hop on the financial scale.

Calculate your annual average spending since you came into your sudden wealth. Then take your portfolio and multiply it by 4%.

This is your distribution rate. It shows if there's excess cash flow above current spending. If you're seeing negative numbers, you have a problem.

Don't know what your annual average spending has been since your financial windfall began? Then you have another problem. As I said before, most people don't know their burn rate, but everyone should.

You need to know what you're spending (and how quickly you're spending it) if you hope to gain any kind of long-term financial stability.

If answering these questions has made you uncomfortable, it's not too late to make a change. You can still fix this. In fact, by reading my book and studying your behaviors, habits, and mindset, you're taking the first step.

From here, I can help you learn how to manage and grow your sudden wealth into lasting wealth. You can stop trading your time for money and start trading it for experiences.

Wealth isn't measured by how much money you earn. It's actually measured by how much you *keep*.

Earned income is the process by which we trade time for money. We spend a great deal of our lives enhancing our skills, academically and/or vocationally, to improve our earning capacity.

But at every turn, someone wants a cut of that. We are tempted with idyllic visions of material goods that will make us happy today, trying to convince us to turn our hard-earned dollars into short-term purchases that depreciate over time (most of them basically immediately). Many of these acquisitions will have very little use or value for us within the year.

Think about the last time that there was something you "needed" to buy. Maybe clothes that were so critical that purchasing them had to happen *right now*. Yet, looking back, you see that the dress, shoes, pants, suit — not to mention the car or boat or whatever it was you were coveting at the moment — no longer had the emotional value you invested in it. How often has this happened to you?

Many people measure success with their income and possessions. I would argue that success is only obtained when transitioning from earned income to "passive income equaling spending."

This is the point of true financial freedom.

The key to opening the door to this kind of liberty is already in your hands. It requires monitoring free cash flow as a percentage of earned income with the intention of creating multiple streams of passive income that equal current earned income.

Yes, that's right. And no, you didn't read that wrong.

If your earned income is $1 million per year, you need to retain enough of that money to put it aside in a passive bucket that will generate multiple other streams of income. This passive income should equal the amount of money you spend and consume. By doing this, you'll unleash a massive shift in the options available to you.

You'll make the leap from trading time for money to trading time for experiences. You'll do things by choice, rather than from need. It's a completely different mindset. I would argue that those high-income earners who don't put enough money into the passive bucket to replace earned income are slaves to their lifestyles. I call them the high-income poor.

I posted some videos about this recently and received some criticism:

"How can you label these people high-income poor?"

Well, here's how: They look good on the outside, but they have little to no financial discipline on the inside. These people's lives will become unraveled during the first economic downturn. Their spending habits and extravagant lifestyles are simply unsustainable.

They viciously consume, consume, consume, and when the economy takes a downward spiral (like in 2008-2009 and 2020), you see their lives crumble very quickly.

There are bankruptcies, divorce, litigation, and sometimes suicide when economic factors (that nobody can predict) surprise even the brightest minds.

There's a very simple way to see where you stand. Just ask yourself this one question:

What percentage of your income do you keep and what percentage do you spend?

For most people, the reality is that at some point — usually very early in the income cycle — we fill our basic needs and then, after that, everything else purchased is a want.

It's reasonable to assume that the more money you make, the higher the percentage of your savings will be. If this isn't the case, and your income increases just to feed your spending, then you're on the elevator going down.

Call it what you want, but it always catches up.

Have an honest conversation with yourself. Go back, look at your spending, and analyze whether or not it tracks with increases in your income. If it does, you need to sit down and figure out how to break the cycle — and fast.

The more money you make as a high-income earner, the more you need to put away, not in specific dollar amounts but as a percentage of what you make. Why? Because the high earner also has a much greater likelihood of experiencing income collapse.

There will eventually be a downturn within your industry, or the world at large, and your income will get caught up in it.

When this happens, it's painful. You'll find yourself selling possessions at the moment when their value is declining. You'll be in a state of forced liquidation. Everyone pays the price, and it affects every aspect of your life: family, kids, career, and social status.

FREE CASH FLOW

If you're not sure where you should be, here are some guidelines. First, if you earn over $250,000 per year, you should think about saving *at least* 30% of your earned income. However, if your income is north of $1 million per year, you should be saving more than 50%. Put it away in that passive bucket.

This whole conversation centers around free cash flow.

It's the single most important aspect of financial literacy. Without it, there's nothing to invest. The balance between spending and free cash flow has to be recognized and understood. If not, you're a ship without a rudder.

The percentage of what's left after spending should always *increase* with income. Such discipline needs to start early.

The solution is to dig into the numbers. See what they say. Spouses, don't bury your head saying you don't understand. Keep asking tough questions until you do understand. You need to know. Get involved and understand the numbers.

You need to take the road to long-term financial health. This requires understanding where you are and where you want to go, then making the necessary decisions to avoid the inevitable pitfalls along the way. The power and control are with you.

With that understood, next I'll guide you through some common traps that will put your financial freedom at risk.

LESSONS AT A GLANCE

- Sudden wealth is often lost as quickly as it was gained if it's not wisely managed.
- Asking what your assets can buy is not the same as knowing what they can support.
- Looking good is perishable.
- People retain wealth not only by understanding finance but also by employing discipline.
- Creating and retaining wealth are two completely different skill sets.
- Know your numbers: What percentage of your income do you keep? What percentage do you spend?

CHAPTER 3
KEEPING WEALTH IS HARDER THAN EARNING IT

"In some cases, I'm not educated enough to do it. In some cases, I'm not smart enough to do it, but I'm smart enough to know what I want and what I don't want. I'm smart enough to know what I can and can't do, and so that's how you have to look at it."

– Dolly Parton

People wonder why I say that holding onto wealth is a lot harder than earning it. It comes down to four financial traps: the popularity trap, the sales trap, the spending trap, and the smart trap. Each trap has the ability to derail your financial gain, which is why it's important to be vigilant and understand the risk involved in each one. In this chapter, we'll explore these traps and how to avoid them.

THE POPULARITY TRAP

Choices and popularity might seem unrelated, but here's the truth: The more money you have, the more choices you have and the more popular you are.

Massive wealth brings out all your "friends," most of whom are just people who want something from you: cash, loans, expensive stuff they can't afford themselves, weekends at your beach house. Whatever they think they can get out of you.

As a therapist whose specialty is working with the super-rich puts it: "I hear this from my clients all the time: 'What do they want from me?'; or 'How are they going to manipulate me?'; or 'They are probably only friends with me because of my money.'"[1]

The best thing you can do — and it's best if you learn this early — is to say the word NO!

This word is at the core of my recommendation that you keep things simple. Don't get into things you don't understand or chase opportunities just because you see others making a lot of money (i.e., crypto, flipping, tech, Mime stock, trading, etc.). In other words, don't get financial FOMO.

When you have wealth, there will always be someone trying to sell you stuff (for their own personal gain) or take money from you (likely because they don't have any).

Of course, there's a time and a place for giving to others, but if you say yes to every person who presents you with an opportunity or asks for money, you won't have anything left to give. When it comes to wealth, it pays to be a little selfish. Keep your best interests in mind, always, even if that makes you unpopular with whoever is wanting a piece of your pie.

As noted in Chapter 2, Dolly Parton is well-known for her philanthropy. She has given away well over 150 million books to schoolchildren through her Imagination Library program. She pays 100% of the college expenses for any of her Dollywood employees who want to pursue a college education.

But she still works from the blueprint her mother provided when she told her daughter: "Always keep something back for you." As Parton explains:

> You can give what you've got, but don't give it all away. I pray also that God will, you know, give me enough to share and enough to spare when it comes to my money, but also to myself. Let me share everything I can, but let me keep me. [2]

With a net worth of around $350 million, Dolly's a woman who has obviously mastered the art of saying "no" … and has therefore built a fortune from which she can say "yes" to quite a lot.

THE SALES TRAP

Understandably, you might be concerned that you'll miss out on some really good deals when it comes to investments — and frankly, you will. But these "really good deals" are also really hard to find.

The good news: You'll miss out on the duds too, and those are a hell of a lot more common than the good stuff.

Take, for example, NBA star Shaquille O'Neal. He's been quite open about learning such lessons the hard way. As he told CNBC:

> When I first came into [the business industry], I lost a lot of money in the 'get rich quick schemes' … from [age] 19 to 26, anybody could come to my office, tell me the deal, and I would take it right away. No research. No due diligence.[3]

What this boils down to is that the game of wealth is a game of odds. It only makes sense to stack the good stuff in your favor.

The reality is that if 10 "opportunities" are presented to you, it's likely that two will be legit and the other eight are merely easy ways to part with your hard-earned money (things like private equity, NFTs, and startups). Most people can't distinguish the good from the bad, so it's imperative you assess the potential risk compared to the potential reward before making a decision.

And the people making the sales pitch? They always make money, whether you win or lose. The only way they *don't* win is if you don't buy what they're selling.

So, how do you avoid the opportunists and the salespeople? I'll be honest, it's hard. It's *really* hard. Everything sounds so good because it's designed to sound really good.

At the time this is being written, George Santos (if that's his real name) is still a member of Congress, representing a Long Island district. He's the guy who lied about … just about everything, from his mom dying in the 9/11 attack (she was in Brazil at the time and didn't pass away until 2016) to having worked for Citigroup and Goldman Sachs (neither company has any record of that). He's been fodder for late-night comedians many times over.

So, it shouldn't be a surprise that what this guy really did for a living was scam people who had come into sudden wealth. In one publicized case, Santos contacted a New York City resident, Christian Lopez, soon after he had been awarded $2 million in damages following a car accident. He invited Lopez to dinner for an investment pitch:

> The 35-year-old Lopez recalled meeting with the embattled congressman at an Italian restaurant in Queens, telling *The Washington Post*, "I felt like we were in 'Goodfellas,' like we were in a mafia movie. They were like, 'Hello, I see you are here with George, right this way.' Bringing us to this fancy restaurant and doing all this, I felt like he was doing it to capture us … He was saying if you give me $300,000, I am going to make you money. I'm going to make you $3 million."[4]

Luckily for Lopez, he realized this all sounded too good to be true. The company that Santos was pitching, Harbor City, had its assets frozen in 2021 and is now under investigation for being a Ponzi scheme.

But if you have sudden wealth, these are the kinds of people who crawl out of the woodwork.

And let's be honest, most of us only understand about 50% of a sales pitch that is targeted at us (and if that's the case, you're actually doing well).

How many times have you bought something only to find out afterward that it didn't do what you thought it did? That what was presented early on never came to fruition?

Of course, the person who sold or pitched you always has a good reason why things didn't work out.

Often, you'll feel stupid for not knowing what you think you should. But it's nearly impossible to know *everything* about products and investments. Not only do salespeople count on that, but they rarely tell you how they get paid. The system is specifically built so it's tough for you to protect yourself.

Purposefully, they'll push the upside while severely soft-pedalling the downside.

Plus, they'll come at you from many different angles, trying to take advantage of weaknesses and catch you when your guard is down. The whole fancy restaurant setup that Santos rolled out is an old gimmick. It's called buttering up the client.

Cold calls are easy enough to get rid of. You can block the number, put yourself on the do-not-call registry, or just don't answer the phone if you don't recognize the number. But then there are friends of friends and, of course, your actual "friends."

It amazes me how money magically affects the number of friends you have. The minute I lost most of my money, most of my so-called friends also vanished.

THE SPENDING TRAP

The temptation to escalate your lifestyle is very, very powerful. People think they need a *better* life with more *stuff* in it.

It's *so* easy to slip into this mentality when you've secured a new client, started your own firm, or picked a good investment that actually paid off big. Your ship has come in. You're finally making a lot of money.

For most people, there's a direct correlation between making a lot of money and living like a movie star. They think they need a massive house, the vacation home, flashy cars, a boat, and maybe even a private plane. It's like they need to show off their good fortune.

They might not be running around showing everyone their bank statements, but … they are.

This isn't a new phenomenon. It's called conspicuous consumption, a term coined in 1899 by economist Thorstein Veblen:

> Conspicuous consumption of valuable goods is a means of reputability to the gentleman of leisure. As wealth accumulates on his hands, his own unaided effort will not avail to sufficiently put his opulence in evidence by this method.[5]

NEW PURCHASES

That language isn't modern but it certainly captures contemporary American culture. To put Veblen's words differently, many people live by the rule of "if you've got it, flaunt it."

However, this is a cycle you can get lost in. The more money you spend, the more addicted you become to spending it.

There are several things at play here — and one is that overly optimistic people think their newfound windfall will continue. As a matter of fact, most people think things will get even better.

So, their optimism fuels their increased spending. Then their lifestyle, surroundings, public image, pressure to succeed, and various other forces (these will be discussed in later chapters) contribute to their overspending.

One surefire way (and a fast one too) to lose your wealth is to just flat-out spend it all. You shouldn't be focused on how many homes, planes, or boats you can buy.

Instead, focus on how much free cash flow you have.

If you're purchasing multiple big-ticket items, especially depreciating assets like a car or boat, it would be a wise move to use cash. In my experience, though, this is generally not what happens.

THE SMART TRAP

When you're successful, there's no reason to think you'll be anything but successful moving forward. This is very common but it's flawed logic. Just because you're knowledgeable, doesn't mean you know it all. And just because you've made some smart decisions to get where you are, doesn't mean your instincts will always pan out.

Here's an ominous lesson illustrating that. I know a family that had a long history in the grocery business. It had been passed down from father to son and included two highly successful specialty stores. They even owned the real estate on which their stores were built. Thanks to smart decisions, they made a good living.

Then they were approached by a salesperson who had vacant property in a nearby town for a third store. Expanding seemed logical — it was an opportunity to enlarge their chain and increase revenue — but in order to build the third store (which would be bigger than the two existing ones), they needed more capital than what they had on hand. They didn't have enough free cash flow.

But they *did* have equity in their homes, business, and land. Leveraging those didn't really seem like a problem. After all, they had a proven track record and had been successful for years.

So they made a classic mistake, one I hope you consider if you're ever in a similar situation and looking to expand a business.

They took on far too much leverage. More than they could actually afford.

They used their money, their own equity, to expand. If they had looked at it objectively, they would have realized that if the third store didn't work out due to some unforeseen market shift or an economic downturn, they were risking their entire net worth.

Because of their track record and the number of years they'd been in business, they could've raised the needed funds using other people's money to finance the third store instead. Sure, they would've given up a percentage of their ownership stake, but they wouldn't have had to put the rest of their business at risk.

Smart people use other people's money to grow their businesses.

There's an abundance of capital out there looking for good business managers. When you have proven success and a good reputation, it's not that difficult to raise money.

Remember, the ultra-poor are hopeful. The ultra-rich are skeptical. This family was blinded by hope in a successful third store and completely overlooked the possibility of failure.

It's so common for people to only look at positive outcomes and not focus on the negative possibilities. But you have to do a full assessment and understand the consequences if the investment fails.

In this case, the salesman they worked with only confirmed the biases of the family (that the third store was a good idea). We can expect this from people who are trying to sell us something.

But there was not anyone within their inner circle that advised them to take a moment and work through the potential downside: They were leveraging everything their parents had worked so hard to build.

Would that conversation have stopped them from making a bad decision? Maybe, maybe not. But it would have at least planted a seed of doubt and perhaps showed them that they hadn't done enough due diligence.

This is where the dilemma of being "too smart" comes in.

You think you know what you're doing, so you don't question your decisions. But it's best to be a little paranoid, to keep that sense of fear and some humility about your skill set. You don't exist in a vacuum.

During the time I was writing this book at the end of 2022 and beginning of 2023, Elon Musk became the poster boy for this kind of "my way or the highway" attitude that can lead to financial pain.

For reasons that are hard to fathom, Musk made an offer of $44 billion for Twitter, way more than it was worth. He apparently figured that out, which is why he tried to back out of the deal. But the mistake was already made. Papers had been signed.

And then, once he got his hands on Twitter, all hell broke loose. Lots of people got fired. Lots of smart people weren't listened to because, if there's one thing you can say about Musk, it's that he's not too humble about his skill set.

Radical changes to the platform he was advised against making — generally by people he soon fired — blew up in his face, including a paid verification system that was a rollout disaster:

Almost immediately, fake verified accounts flooded the platform. An image of Mario giving the middle finger from what looked like the official Nintendo account stayed up for more than a day. An account masquerading as the drug manufacturer Eli Lilly tweeted that insulin would now be free. Company executives begged Twitter to take down the tweet ...

Days after the subscription service debuted, Twitter canned it ...

Musk's blundering left a deep scar. Twitter Blue was meant to begin shifting Twitter's revenue away from ads toward subscriptions. But while chasing a relatively paltry new cash stream, Musk torched the company's ad business — the source of the vast majority of its billions in revenue.[6]

Musk had overseen the growth of two wildly successful businesses, Tesla and SpaceX. But neither of their income streams depended on maintaining relationships with advertisers. The value of Twitter has plummeted and it has dragged down the value of Tesla too, which is a brand that was heavily dependent on Musk having a good reputation.

If the richest guy in the world can make assumptions about what he knows and how "smart" he is, then you can too.

The economic climate fluctuates over time. There will be disruptions or market shifts you cannot possibly see coming. It doesn't mean you're not smart. That's just how it is. So, if you walk into each transaction with a healthy sense of paranoia and fear, along with a humble heart, you'll make better long-term decisions.

A common misconception investors make is that success or intelligence in one area will translate to successful investment decisions.

Consider retired MLB pitcher Curt Schilling. His career earnings over 19 years were $115 million.

Upon retirement in 2006, Schilling invested $50 million in a video game company, 38 Studios, helping bring the company to Rhode Island in an effort to create jobs and offset the state's high unemployment rate. But on July 7, 2012, 38 Studios declared bankruptcy. This included the company leaving the state of Rhode Island, which had also made loans to the company of about $112 million.[7]

After this, Schilling reverted to broadcasting as a way to stay afloat financially — before getting fired by ESPN for controversial social media posts — and now he's paying the bills as a conservative media gadfly.

The takeaway here is that you're not as smart as you think you are.

And it would behoove you to understand that salespeople are more knowledgeable than you.

If you disagree, I think you're in trouble. If you agree, there's hope for you yet.

As much as I know about the investment world and private transactions, I'm always amazed at what I don't know (but I thought I did). I've been in this line of work for decades, and there are still plenty of things I don't know. So, if you've had less experience and you're jumping into a new investment, there are many reasons to be skeptical.

Salespeople are going to present you with a lot of information, but be wary.

They have the advantage. They will show you what they want you to see, emphasizing the benefits. They can also frame a situation so that you actually view the information through the lens they want you to use. Buying tires? The cost becomes secondary when someone asks: "How much would you pay for peace of mind about the security of your children in the car?"

The solution is to always be pessimistic about new investments.

Being overly optimistic about your finances is the easiest way to lose more than you ever thought possible. Estimate conservatively. Place your bets on a low-end return.

And always *focus on what you can lose* and how doing so will affect the long-term. If you can stomach the potential loss and still like the investment, then it's reasonable to move forward. But you *must* focus on the risk first.

Being skeptical, wanting more information, and pausing to see the bigger picture doesn't make you a negative person. It's a smart practice that clears the way to follow, and protect, the path to positive gains.

The quicker you realize you can't depend on the rosy outlook that salespeople present, and that you don't know everything, the better off you'll be.

KEEP IT SIMPLE

Throughout this book, we discuss the benefits of simple asset allocation and using passive investment vehicles to grow your wealth. Beyond that, you're just rebalancing parameters and leaving everything alone.

However, the vast majority of people just can't seem to buy into this simple, yet effective, method. They're trying to outsmart the market. What they usually end up doing is causing themselves a great deal of pain by making mistakes.

Here are some of the most common missteps:

Trying to Time the Market

This is a surefire way of flushing money down the toilet. What feels good or right at the moment is often the wrong decision. Staying the course has always delivered better results.

Reaching for Yield

People are often not happy with current rates of return on safe investments, so they look around for something that pays a better yield, and of course, an investment adviser can always find something to sell them. But think about the trade-off. Did you get a higher yield or did you just take on more risk? Generally, the answer is that you're taking on more risk. And most people simply don't realize how much.

Short-Term Focus on Long-Term Goals

You need to understand you're not following a one-year plan. It's a 20-, 30-, or 40-year investment process. It's incredibly important to build in long-term, consistent returns that avoid big losses over your life. You can't panic because of a short-term event and sell off your investments. Doing so could dramatically affect your long-term wealth.

Making Adjustments During a Market Crisis

Remember what happened to the markets during the financial crisis of 2008-2009? It didn't matter if you owned real estate or stocks, everything went down *significantly*. COVID-19 unleashed a whole host of economic gyrations. However, if you were able (and willing) to stay the course, your investments probably looked pretty good once the markets recovered. Consistency of investments leads to longevity of wealth, so keep it simple and don't let your fear take over during a market crisis.

Buying Yesterday's Winners

Some people just can't help themselves. They have to chase the hot new investment trend rather than something that's proven steady over a longer period of time. Looking at past short-term performance, where you make decisions based on how well something has done in the last five years, is a big mistake. There are far too many additional considerations that go into an investment decision that get overlooked when people follow this mentality.

Too Much Leverage

In the earlier grocery store example, a real estate project was undertaken with a high element of leverage. Both the market and the business climate were good. Because everything seemed to be fine, the family entered into the agreement feeling like all the bases were covered. They thought it was a solid deal. Instead, they lost the family business — and much more.

Investors can access real estate in a variety of ways, usually through partnerships or limited partnerships. But some own real estate directly and have enough financial resources to buy office and industrial buildings. Unfortunately, they often don't do a proper analysis of what would happen during a market downturn when taking on the leverage the project requires.

Before entering into any new investment, you should stress test the scenario. Get a handle on where you'd be if things go south.

Let's look back at the 2008 housing crisis. The people who got into real trouble had too much leverage (they borrowed too much relative to the size of their assets). On the opposite end of the spectrum, people who did not have as much leverage experienced property declines, but they didn't lose everything. They had the financial power to sit tight through the bottom of the cycle.

Ten years later, many properties were back to peak value levels. But during the crisis, it was very painful for people to sit back, be patient, and weather the storm.

When investing, it's crucial to look at every angle and fully understand where you'd be financially if the worst happens.

Capital Calls: Having to Put in More Money

Another key point regarding real estate and private partnerships that most people don't anticipate is something called a capital call. This is when an investment loses momentum and the general partner comes back to the existing investor group to ask for more money (which is well within his or her right).

This is a very difficult decision to make: put more money in or lose face. Putting in more funding completely changes the parameters of the initial investment. There's no correct universal answer since each situation is different, but in every scenario you need to do your analysis upfront and measure the likelihood that you'll eventually have to put additional money into a project. Remember, things *always* cost more and take longer than you expect.

Not Controlling Investment Fees

It's important to understand that the deck is stacked against you. The sooner you figure that out, the better. In a just world, compensation for financial professionals, especially investment advisers, should have some standards or guidelines regarding how they get paid, but this isn't the case.

Fees range widely, from annual to upfront commissions to back-end incentives. Often, fees come in many layers.

When you don't understand these fee structures, you don't know the right questions to ask, nor are you in a position to effectively negotiate.

You're coming at it from the weak side, and the weak side always pays more.

The other key issue is that investments and costs are not uniform, meaning that different products pay different levels of fees and commissions. Of course, this makes it difficult to get unbiased advice.

So, how do you know what to look for? How can you protect yourself?

There's only one way: Ask your adviser to put everything in writing. Once you can see it all on paper, you can ask if there are other solutions that cost less and get those in writing as well. This shows your adviser that you'll be paying close attention and following up on them. It changes the game and holds the adviser accountable.

My point is that you must determine what the total cost of investment fees will be ahead of time. This includes manager fees, trading costs, investment adviser fees, custodial fees, and any product-specific fees and commissions.

Finally, make sure you do an annual review with your adviser. You should fully understand total annual costs. If you don't, or the information seems fishy, ask questions.

Misunderstanding Risk

In my own case, I made the classic mistake of greatly underestimating the amount of risk I was taking on, and that led to a battle with the SEC. And just like with the IRS, you go into a fight with the SEC as a decided underdog.

As I discussed in Chapter 1, I was targeted for conducting a principal transaction. I was selling a security, which is a financial interest in something that I owned. I'd never done that before, so this was uncharted territory where I had very little experience or understanding.

What I didn't realize (and wasn't advised on) was the complexity and heightened level of scrutiny I was taking on with everything I did when entering a principal transaction.

If I would have taken a hard look at the risk-reward situation and determined the benefit to me and my clients in terms of dollars — and the corresponding risk if we didn't get it right — I would have never, *ever* done it. But all I could see was cashing in on a successful investment decision.

I didn't look at how badly things could turn out if it *wasn't* successful.

I had advisers and lawyers helping me through this process. But nobody insisted I look at the risk-reward scenarios, and I faithfully trusted the people leading the process.

But there's a reason why nobody asked me to cross-check the risk and reward. In many cases, it's because people don't get paid unless a transaction occurs. Lawyers get paid for their services upon completion of a deal. Advisers get a cut of your sale. So, by the very nature of the investment environment, the information you receive is skewed.

It's *your* responsibility to flesh out what can go wrong by asking the tough questions and being willing to listen to the answers. This is an important part of being able to do an honest assessment. The first four questions should be the following:

- What happens if this doesn't work out?
- If we screw this up, what happens to me personally?
- What happens to my money if this doesn't go well?
- Will I have to put more money into the deal at some point?

I'm a huge advocate of simplicity; I *know* it can help you cultivate better judgment. One of the easiest ways to accurately assess an investment decision is to put a line down the middle of a piece of paper and make a pros and cons list.

On the pros side, note all the positive possibilities. On the cons side, describe the tiered consequences of what might happen if things don't go well.

If I had done this simple task when considering selling my business, I would have realized two things: If I got the transaction right, I could capture the benefit of selling 10% of my interest in the business, but if I got it wrong, I risked everything. The problem lied in the fact that I wasn't aware of this; I never considered the ramifications of getting it wrong.

If I brought this idea of selling my firm as a principal transaction to 10 people in 10 different industries, laid out the risk-reward, and asked them for their advice, they'd all tell me not to do it.

And yet, I did it.

I'm an industry professional, yet I made the classic mistake so many people make every single day. And the reason I did it was that I never wrote out that cons column.

I never assessed the risks.

I focused only on the pros, which reinforced my desire to go through with the deal.

Another simple way to assess an investment decision is this: If you can live with the negative ramifications, then you're OK with the positive side. But if you can't live with the negative outcome, then you don't get the positive outcome either. If I had understood this, I wouldn't have made the choice I did.

Let's look at one more example. I know the owner of a real estate firm who not only bought a huge piece of property but also got a loan because there were lots of different developers who wanted to buy sections of the property. The loan would help them cover their costs while the developers worked out their own purchasing deals.

The real estate firm had most of the property "spoken for" before they actually bought it, so they didn't feel like there was a lot of risk. But the issue was that the developers didn't have any money that was actually *committed*. They had just voiced their "interest."

It should go without saying that interest and commitment are two very different things.

They finally closed on the property right before the 2008 downturn, at which point the developers disappeared. The firm that bought the property was stuck with it — and the big loan.

After the downturn, they went into foreclosure (like so many others) because they were on the hook for a massive amount of money that they couldn't come up with. The landowner was sued personally and ended up not only losing the property, but also a significant portion of his own fortune and suffering severe damage to his business reputation.

Real estate can make you a fortune, but it can also cost you your fortune.

Keep in mind that the more complex the situation (i.e., the more money you have in investments), the more you open yourself up to mistakes and what I call "got you" moments. You'll recognize these moments when you find yourself saying you didn't think what happened was possible.

And when something goes wrong, it's your fault, not the person who put the deal together. Then you're the one who suffers while they get paid regardless. Sure, you can sue them if they mess it up, but that's expensive and a long, drawn-out process. Why go down that road when it's all avoidable?

These are the things you need to consider when opportunity strikes. Don't think it can't go wrong simply because other people have done something similar successfully. People, including you, make bad decisions when under pressure.

If you've already had this painful experience, this chapter will likely make you sick to your stomach. Others will read this in disbelief, only to fall prey to the various traps at some point in the future. Hopefully, others will read this and take heed.

The game is not won by taking on a ton of risk. The game is won by not losing your money.

LESSONS AT A GLANCE

- Protect your capital first.
- When expanding, try to use other people's money.
- Salespeople are not on your side. They make money only when you buy something from them.
- You must educate yourself on each aspect of every investment.
- If you don't understand an investment, don't do it.

- Conduct a stress test on each investment. How much can you stand to lose? What happens to you if it doesn't work out?
- Get everything in writing — it protects you.

CHAPTER 4
ADVICE FOR
ATHLETES: KEEP YOUR WINDFALL

"I thought I knew and trusted some of my peeps. The good news is I've finally found people that are trustworthy and I'm a little smarter. As an athlete you don't learn all these things. You're just focused on training."

– Dorothy Hamill

Professional athletes are often an extreme example of over-spenders. They come into sudden wealth after growing up seeing a lifestyle they wanted to replicate and immediately begin living it without realizing what it takes to sustain that level of spending.

Others are simply not thinking far enough into the future. We'll use athletes because their example is so extreme, but if you look at your own life you may see similar patterns of behavior as the concepts outlined in this chapter truly apply to anyone. Looking at these through the lens of an athlete provides a clear picture of the effect of sudden wealth and how what you do with it can make or break you. This is because there are very few professions that have such sharp limitations on career span fused with offering such high salaries.

Because of this (and exorbitant spending behaviors), athletes are exceedingly likely to lose every dollar they've earned and then some.

Athletes have multiple forces working against them:

- They came into sudden wealth (which you've already learned is extremely easy to squander).
- They have an extremely short period of time in which they can earn a lot of money and fill a deep asset bucket that can sustain them over the long-term.
- They have trouble separating what they want to spend versus what they can spend (in many cases because of peer pressure or a desire to keep up with the Joneses).
- They are overly optimistic about their career and earning potential.
- They delegate too much control.
- They are more concerned with looking good rather than long-term financial health.

- They often lack financial literacy, which makes them vulnerable to the sales trap.

Another significant factor is that athletes are usually quite young when they come into their sudden wealth. It's a lot to ask people in their early twenties — and in some cases still teenagers — to be responsible with a giant pile of cash. Many of the kids being drafted into the big leagues didn't come from money and they don't know how to deal with it when they get it.

It's not their fault — it's just that no one ever taught them.

And, of course, athletes tend to be very optimistic. After all, they *have to be* to get to where they are. You don't get to the pros by thinking you'll never make it. You can't compete at a high level if you don't think you're going to succeed.

This positive attitude leads them to believe they'll get contract after contract, that they won't get hurt, and that their careers will be more like LeBron James (20 years into a historic career and the first active NBA player to become a billionaire) than Ryan Leaf (the second overall pick in the 1998 NFL draft behind Peyton Manning who quickly washed out of the league and was soon in legal trouble).

But the reality of the situation is that professional athletes are unlikely to get a second, much less a third, contract. Of the top three major professional sports in America (football, basketball, and baseball), baseball has the longest average career, at just 5.6 years.[1] Athletes will earn a high income for what's likely to be an extremely short period of time. And how they live afterward is 100% dependent upon their lifestyle choices and financial decisions during their brief career.

So, what happens when an overly optimistic person comes into a ton of money and is ill-prepared to deal with it?

Well, someone like this is extremely vulnerable to the sales community. They are like prey to a predator. They also focus on the wrong thing: what money can buy instead of what it can support.

HBO's show *Ballers*, which ran for two seasons in 2015-2016, takes viewers into the world of hotshot NFL stars and their flashy lifestyles. Between its smart casting, whip-sharp banter, and lush locations, *Ballers* provides binge-worthy entertainment.

I'd also argue that the writers were telling a cautionary tale about the dangers of fast money and the lure of lavish lifestyles. If you look closely, *Ballers* lets its characters make poor decisions.

At the heart of the show is Spencer Strasmore, a former NFL superstar turned asset manager. Spencer, played by the charismatic Dwayne "The Rock" Johnson, wants to keep his crew of young NFL stars from making terrible financial decisions. He counsels them, and they ignore him.

Throughout the first season, viewers slowly come to learn that Spencer has a secret. When he was younger, he got his friends to invest in a real estate scheme and he lost everyone's money, including much of his own. Now, he's trying to fix those mistakes by being a financial mentor to young players, trying to help them not make the same mistakes he did. Does he succeed? Sometimes he does, sometimes he doesn't.

The reason I'm bringing up *Ballers* is that its writing beautifully illustrates a very common occurrence.

A lot of professional athletes are what I call "ultra-poor."

It may not appear that way with the sports cars, mansions, and bling, but it's true. They're poor.

Too often, young athletes sign a large contract with a hefty signing bonus and then buy into a luxurious lifestyle, which they often share generously with friends and family. That last part is honorable, but it's the wrong decision for their long-term financial health.

According to *Sports Illustrated*, "By the time they have been retired for two years, 78% of former NFL players have gone bankrupt or are under financial stress because of joblessness or divorce."[2]

Furthermore, a paper published by the National Bureau of Economic Research states that "the bankruptcy proportion increases steadily up to 15.7% at 12 years of retirement."[3]

Considering that the average NFL career only lasts 3.3 years,[4] a lot of NFL players are retiring from the sport in their mid-twenties and they're bankrupt by their mid-to-late-thirties.

And, of course, this trend is not exclusive to the NFL. According to the same *Sports Illustrated* study:

"Within five years of retirement, an estimated 60% of former NBA players are broke."

Basketball icon Allen Iverson, an 11-time NBA All-Star,[5] is believed to have notched a $154.5 million salary, plus more in endorsement deals, over the course of his 15 seasons. But, according to *The Washington Post* reporter Kent Babb's book *Not A Game*, Iverson was soon borrowing money from friends. Even his wife, Tawanna, was visiting pawn shops and consignment stores to try to sell her jewelry[6] (though Iverson has repeatedly denied claims of financial troubles[7]).

And MLB players fall prey to this lifestyle as well. Center fielder Lenny Dykstra played 12 seasons with the Mets and Phillies. After retiring at age 33 in 1996, it seemed as though Dykstra was going to end up a wealthy man. In 2008, he was reportedly worth more than $58 million.[8] But just one year later, Dykstra filed bankruptcy, claiming $31 million in liabilities with just $50,000 in assets.[9]

DON'T BE THE BROKE SPORTS STAR

Just like anything else in this world, making the right choices depends on context and perspective.

Professional athletes, when they realize their athletic abilities can (and will) deteriorate, should take the first step to become ultra-rich.

Ultra-rich athletes as well as artists, musicians, and other professionals who come into sudden wealth understand there's a short window in which they'll perform at the highest level. They also know that earning millions of dollars is incredibly difficult outside of their specific skill set.

Athletes might earn $3 million per year and then — depending on education, investments, and other choices — bring in between $50,000 and $200,000 per year for the rest of their lives (and sometimes even less). That's a life-changing drop in salary. The ultra-rich athlete knows this *will* happen and plans accordingly.

Ironically, an athlete who didn't fall into this trap is one who entered the NBA straight out of high school at age 18 and then enjoyed (still is, in fact) an unusually long career. In 2023, he's still playing at an All-Star level. And he just broke Kareem Abdul-Jabbar's all-time points record.

And as already mentioned, another record he has already set is being the first active NBA player to become a billionaire.

Yes, LeBron James has made hundreds of millions in salary and endorsement deals, but he's also been a savvy investor. He co-founded a sports nutrition company (Beachbody) with Arnold Schwarzenegger, owns a stake in Blaze Pizza, and his multi-sector SpringHill Company is worth about $300 million.[10]

Like Dolly Parton, Lebron has always been openly ambitious regarding his business pursuits, so much so that he's also followed a long-term plan to make them happen.

How'd he do this? He analyzed the situation:

> "I know that once I get off the floor, there's going to be more of my time spent off than on," he says. "So from age 9 to — if you make it to 40 — that's 31 years of your life. But from 40 to 85 or 90 - hopefully I'm lucky to get to 90 — that's 50 years. I still have to live life, beyond the hardwood."[11]

None other than the Oracle of Omaha, Warren Buffet, had this to say about LeBron:

> People really do have minds that function better than other people's in certain areas that you can't give a test for. And LeBron, in addition to a lot of other talents, he has a money mind. And he gets stuff … He can separate out the cream from the crap, and you get more of the latter proposed to you than you do of the former. You really have to be able to suss it out.[12]

When you go from living on a scholarship to signing a professional contract, you have so many commas and zeros in your bank account that your head spins with possibilities. Real estate agents, car dealerships, and luxury goods purveyors seem to put you on speed dial. It's easy to find yourself sucked into the gravitational pull of buying into the grand life so many of your peers are living.

It's clear that LeBron has resisted that to a great extent, which is really impressive since he signed an $18.8 million NBA contract when he was only 19 (after he had signed a deal with Nike at age 18) and first played in Cleveland near his hometown of Akron:

He's careful with his money and even his former teammates count on him for money advice. He and his teammates have even been known to split the bill at dinner. Player Iman Shumper said, "We're smart about our coins, man. If I ever wanted to have someone on the team invest my money, it'd be LeBron."[13]

Not everyone is LeBron. As we've already covered, few players have careers like his. The average NBA career lasts about 4.5 years, not over 20. And given that only a select few athletes play for over a decade, the majority of players are in the league for only a year or two.

Managing Your Money When You're Not LeBron

What's my advice if you're not LeBron (even though we've established there are traits of his that are worth emulating)?

In a nutshell, don't do much.

What am I suggesting?

Don't buy a single thing.

I can hear you say: What do you mean? I can't buy a new car or a house? I can't give back to my neighborhood?

Consider this from Abdul-Jabbar:

> People who work for the retired players' associations of the various pro leagues often find the former athletes living with parents or in cars or — in one troubling instance — under a bridge overpass. Recently, someone I have worked with noticed a former NFL great employed in the baggage room at a hotel. These sad tales should serve as cautionary stories for the present crop of pro jocks, but it seems the bad news does not cause many of them to pay heed and wise up.[14]

It's not just sports stars who make bad choices, of course. Celebrities and rich people of all kinds commonly mismanage their money. And, well, everyone else too.

A 2017 issue of *New York Magazine* featured a candid description of an accountant who tries to advise wealthy clients:

> I had one client who wanted to buy a property. I said, "It's a really bad idea. You don't have enough money. You can barely scrape together the down payment. The monthly mortgage is going to kill you. You're going to have a lot of upkeep. Don't do it." They called my partner, who said, "Don't do it." They called someone else, "Don't do it." Called someone else, "That's a bad idea." Called their agent, "Oh, yeah, do it. Go ahead. I'll get you more work." They just keep going until they find someone who says yes. But it's my job to sometimes say it's not okay, and here's why. We try to rein them in.[15]

There will be an appropriate time and place to buy a home and a car and build a legacy of philanthropy. But at the start of a sports career, you need to focus on your athletic earning potential, your finances, and saving for the future.

When your career ends, these early moves will sustain you forever.

Your earning potential as an athlete depends upon doing everything possible to make sure you're taking care of your body as an income generator. Partying, eating junk food, and skipping training camp all diminish your ability to earn during your short career, so your athletic skills and physical health need to be your top priority.

Next, it's crucial to start your professional life with a modest lifestyle:

- Live simply for a few years so you can invest properly.
- Rent your home rather than buying a massive mansion.
- Buy a used car (or better yet, keep your old one if it's still running well).
- Don't give money away (people are going to come out of the woodwork asking for it).
- If you're eating out with LeBron, split the tab.

Even the most talented players don't play forever. Once that youth and vitality are gone, they'll need their savings to maintain their lifestyle. The moves made at 22 will dictate the next 50 years. LeBron got that.

Take a minute to think about what you'd like those years to look like.

A TALE OF TWO PLAYERS

Now, let's take a look at two proverbial players: Gary and Mark.

Both sign similar $2 million per year NBA deals for three years. After taxes, that's $83,000 per month each year.

Ultra-poor Gary

First, let's take Gary. He is thrilled about his new professional life and optimistic about having a long career in the top tier of the league.

ULTRA-POOR GARY

		Running Balance
Starting Balance	$2,000,000	
Taxes	($1,000,000)	$1,000,000
Down Payment	($500,000)	$500,000
Mortgage	($144,000)	$356,000
Car	($80,000)	$276,000
Gifts	($80,000)	$196,000
Wardrobe	($100,000)	$96,000
Annual Expenses	($120,000)	-$24,000
Starting Balance	$2,000,000 CONTRACT	
Ending Balance	-$24,000 IN DEBT	

As explained, Gary's net pay comes out to $83,000 per month. But he never actually considers his net pay, so he spends himself into a $2 million per year lifestyle without really thinking about what that means.

First, he buys a $2.5 million home with $500,000 down, which means a $12,000 monthly mortgage. He buys the fancy new sports car he's always wanted … and an SUV. He gets a new wardrobe (complete with a Rolex) to match his sophisticated new lifestyle.

That first $2 million is already long gone — and then some.

At the end of the contract's first year, Gary has no savings. In fact, he has negative savings and credit card debt.

The following year, Gary manages to save only $33,000, which he funnels into a portfolio totaling $792,000.

What's important here is that if he doesn't get another contract, which is not at all unusual, then Gary will be trying to sell his house while he looks for a job.

How can that be? Let's round up and say his portfolio is worth $800,000. This amount will only generate about $35,000 per year in returns, meaning he can't even afford his mortgage payments, let alone the rest of his lifestyle.

His cars will be repossessed within a few months, and he'll be in a pawn shop trying to get a decent deal for that Rolex.

The luxurious lifestyle that Gary was so excited to experience wasn't sustainable.

Although $2 million per year *sounds* like a lot of money, remember it's only $1 million after taxes and basic expenses (agents don't pay themselves). And it's easy to blow through that and end up left with absolutely nothing to show for your hard work. Gary's mindset wasn't in the right place, which led to financially reckless behavior.

It's painful to go backward, but that's always the path of the ultra-poor. Believe me, I've done it.

It hurts in every possible way: your relationships, your status in the community, and your own self-worth all suffer under the extreme stress.

But you can avoid this with the ultra-rich mindset.

Now, let's contrast this example with Mark's story.

Ultra-rich Mark

Same contract, same money. But Mark is focused on moving forward, growing his wealth, and setting himself up for financial freedom.

ULTRA-RICH MARK

		Running Balance
Starting Balance	$2,000,000	
Taxes	($1,000,000)	$1,000,000
Down Payment	$0	$1,000,000
Car	($30,000)	$970,000
Gifts	$0	$970,000
Wardrobe	$0	$970,000
Annual Expenses	($90,000)	$880,000
Starting Balance	**$2,000,000 CONTRACT**	
Ending Balance	**$880,000 SAVED**	

Mark buys a $30,000 used car and rents a townhouse for $3,000 per month. He spends $7,500 each month after taxes and saves the rest. That gives him around $75,500 per month to put in his asset bucket.

Over his 36-month contract, his asset bucket grows to $3 million. Even if Mark never gets another contract, he should be able to receive $110,000 in income per year forever from his portfolio generating income.

When you're dealing with a three-year contract, the correct strategy is to stash enough money away in a portfolio so it can continue to support that same *moderate* lifestyle for the rest of your life. If Mark doesn't get another contract, he still gets that $110,000 per year.

The main goal is to put enough money away so that, in the event you're not offered another contract, you can live on what you've already earned. And if you do get another contract, simply repeat the process.

Over the course of a three-year contract, you need to save 45% after taxes to be able to replace that income later on. In total, you're only spending 7% of the annual contract. It's particularly important to save this much because the contracts (and sometimes, careers) are so short — you have less time to save, but you also have less time to correct mistakes.

THE SAVINGS-ASSETS-REPLACEMENT-SPENDING WHEEL

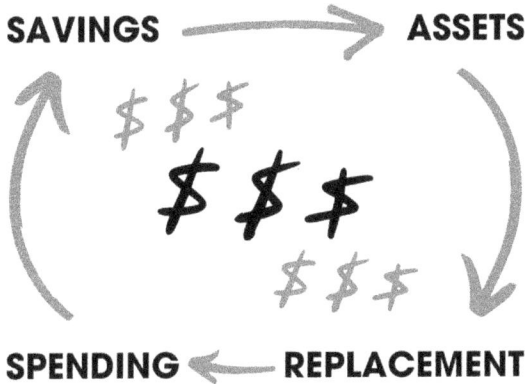

SAVINGS ⟶ ASSETS

$ $ $

$ $ $

$ $ $

SPENDING ⟵ REPLACEMENT

Meet the savings-assets-replacement-spending wheel. Memorize it. Burn it into your brain.

When used correctly, it is the foundation of becoming ultra-rich, whether you're a professional athlete or not. It's the foundation of building wealth, a tool that helps you visualize your money as constantly working in your favor. Too often, people don't take the time to think about how saved money turns into something else: assets.

Money stockpiled away isn't static. When handled properly, savings multiply until they become actual assets that replace your earned income. This frees up your time to do the things you actually want to do in retirement, as opposed to taking that job in the baggage room at a hotel.

Mark structures his spending to reflect his income in the event he doesn't get a second contract. The struggle for Mark will lie with any envy he feels toward Gary's lifestyle. But if Mark stays focused on his goal and continually makes choices to support it, he has a long-term plan for living the same lifestyle later on, rather than having short-term fun followed by years of money struggles and poverty.

This is the essence of the ultra-rich mindset.

You have to ask yourself: Which lifestyle would you rather have? While it may seem like Gary has the upper hand initially, it's really Mark who's in control. Gary has a plan for today, whereas Mark has a 50-year vision.

The harsh reality of this situation is that very few athletes sign a second contract. Professional sports are hyper competitive and tough on the body (your primary asset in this scenario).

By the end of a player's first contract, younger athletes have entered the draft class and are working hard to take your job. And from the owners' perspectives, they'll do it for less money, which very well may mean you're out of a job.

So, consider the following: Can you replace your income and maintain your lifestyle?

Mark can, but Gary can't. Gary never created a sufficient asset bucket.

Let's fast-forward to the end of their contracts: Each is fortunate enough to sign another deal worth $12 million for three years. So, $4 million per year.

Mark continues to live his same frugal lifestyle (which would be considered luxurious to most people). He uses the same formula of savings versus spending, living on $280,000 per year before taxes, with his lifestyle spending essentially doubled by the new contract. At the same time, he's increasing his asset bucket contributions.

Following his second contract, Mark could buy a home that would keep him within the $22,500 monthly budget. He gives himself a raise (and perhaps treats himself to a vacation or a nicer car) but his raise is directly proportional to his replacement plan. He continues to put the majority of his income into his asset bucket.

At the end of the second contract, Mark has $6.4 million saved. As long as he stays within his $280,000 per year budget, he can live on this amount forever.

But for guys like Gary, what generally happens is they continue to spend at the same rate, and probably dial things up a notch. Gary doesn't put a significant amount into his asset bucket, which means he'll always have a dramatic imbalance between spending and assets.

The minute the music stops, he's in big trouble. At the end of his contract, he has very little cash saved. The meager savings he did manage to accumulate will quickly vanish if he attempts to maintain his lavish lifestyle after retirement, which comes at him fast before the age of 30.

There are two basic mistakes here.

As we discussed in Chapter 2, when sudden wealth hits it's easy to focus on what it can buy right now, rather than what it can support in the future.

The second mistake has to do with over-optimism.

Athletes, as a group, tend to think they won't get hurt or that their skills will not deteriorate. Of course, the reality is that most athletes *will* suffer some sort of injury and their bodies *will* age, quickly, making it more and more difficult to perform at the highest level. As much as they might not want to think about the end of their careers, not everyone will be like Tom Brady, who was somehow still a top quarterback at age 45, or LeBron still going strong while pushing 40.

To put it simply: Take any rise in income slowly. Be pessimistic. Assume you'll get hurt. Assume every contract is your last. And if you do get resigned, funnel excess amounts into your asset bucket and keep your living expenses low.

What you need to calculate is how much you have to save to replicate your current lifestyle … forever.

How big does your asset bucket need to be by the end of your contract?

You need to decide how you want to live for the rest of your life. Do you want to live large on $250,000 for five years and then pare back to $30,000 in year six? Or are you alright with living off $90,000 (like Mark) for a few years so you can live like this forever?

I completely understand that it takes a tremendous amount of discipline and self-sacrifice to live conservatively when you're earning a lot of money. But you *need* to find a way to do this for yourself and your family.

Otherwise, you'll be desperate for a job within a few years of retirement, and it won't be one with anything like the yearly income you just squandered.

Your Ultimate Goal

From a distance, this advice seems practical, maybe even obvious. It's easy to look at other people's mistakes and see where they went wrong. And although this chapter focuses on athletes, the advice is universal.

These are lessons for everyone, not just suddenly wealthy athletes.

You should save in relation to your income, especially if you're working on contracts with no guarantee of renewal. In a sense, no job is forever, whether you own a business or you're employed by a corporation. The reality is that you don't know what curveballs the future may throw at you, so it's important to save enough to replace future earned income.

There were a lot of secretaries and support staff who worked at Enron when it went belly up.[16] They went down with the ship too.

As you move up in your career, you must be mindful not to overspend and undersave.

Also, consider the pace of job changes in today's tech-driven economy.

For example, in the 1980s through to the early 2000s, pagers were a big deal. Plenty of people had them so they could be "paged" wherever they were in case of an emergency. Remember, this was before the cell phones were a thing. But as cell phone use increased, pagers took a nosedive. Today, physicians are about the only people still using them.

What if you owned a chain of pager stores? You would have experienced a few years of massive sales and impressive, steady income.

But what happened when cell phones became common consumer items? Your income would have declined dramatically.

The same is true for brick-and-mortar stores like Circuit City, Borders Books & Music, Radio Shack, or FYE. With the rise streaming apps like Spotify and services like Amazon, people don't have to go to stores to find the stuff they want. They can stream or download their music, read a book on their tablet, and have products shipped straight to their door.

The CEOs of these companies (and many others like them) have suffered the same fate as athletes who ran wild with their lifestyle early on. And if those CEOs accelerated their lifestyle in relation to their short-term income windfall, they were in rough shape when the decline hit.

My main point is that careers go hot and cold.

It's not a matter of *if* but *when*. You have to prepare for the cold. Understanding free cash flow and the importance of transferring funds into your asset bucket will make the cold spells in your career feel a little less frigid.

The math is the same. Regardless of how you came into your money, you can apply this information to your own life. You simply *never* know when your income bubble will burst, so you have to take advantage of it while you can, which is what athletes so often get so horribly wrong.

The ultimate goal is longevity of income.

Anyone can follow this systematic process but athletes, in particular, *need* to because they're dealing with such a short period of earning and such small margins of error. They typically need to make three to five years of income last at least 50 to 60 years. If they save like they're supposed to, they can set themselves up for life.

If you take nothing else from this book, remember this: Every earner needs to make a decision about their spending.

Are you going to figure out how much you *can* spend? Or are you going to just spend whatever you want and not think about the consequences?

Yes, of course you want to get rid of your crappy old car and get a fancy one. Of course, you want a bigger house (or any house at all). And anyone would want to pay off their mom's debt after all she's done for them.

But right this instant is not the time to do it. You need to make your asset bucket your absolute top priority. Later on, when your financial future is stable, you can loosen the purse strings (but only a little).

Athlete or not, we all have a period in our lives where we catch the financial upwind and see an increase in income. It may not necessarily be the increase athletes experience, but you get my point. So, think back and ask yourself how you handled it. If that windfall hasn't come yet, it will. What will you do when it happens?

LESSONS AT A GLANCE

- Sacrifice early to enjoy longevity.
- Make sure short-term and long-term goals are aligned.
- When a contract is short, the savings rate must be higher.
- Freedom happens when earned income is replaced by passive income.
- The higher the income, the greater the savings rate.
- If you radically increase spending when newfound wealth happens, in no time at all you're going to end up in a vicious cycle of never having enough money.
- Work toward replacing income with your asset bucket.
- Freeze spending at current levels.
- When you get a raise, keep expenses where they are and save the new income.
- These lessons apply to everyone.

CHAPTER 5
AVOID FEAR AND
GREED AT ALL COSTS

"If you lose self-control, everything will fall."

– John Wooden

The advertised return on an investment will always be more than what you actually get. The reasons? Customary costs, taxation, and more than anything, investment behavior.

This difference between an investment and investor return is often called the behavior gap.

As much as we'd all like to believe we're completely rational people with a firm grip on our emotions, we're just as likely to throw all that rationale out the window when we're scared. And on the opposite end of the spectrum, when we're being greedy we find foolhardy courage we never thought we had.

The problem with these very common, very human emotions is that they can get us into a lot of trouble, especially in the world of investing.

When the market is consumed by fear, Wall Street promotes safety in the form of selling: "Get out before you lose everything!" When greed is in, the Street says buy, buy, buy: "This stock is really hot, you should get in while you can still afford to."

Billionaire Warren Buffett executes the exact opposite approach:

> Two super-contagious diseases, fear and greed, will forever occur in the investment community. The timing of these epidemics will be unpredictable ... We simply attempt to be fearful when others are greedy and to be greedy only when others are fearful.[1]

If you were to walk through your front door and find your living room on fire, what would you do? Rational people would call the fire department. You'd hope that strategy would make sense to everyone.

But, for some reason, when it comes to our hard-earned savings, that's not how we put out the fire. Oftentimes when the market is in a downward trajectory, our irrational side does the thinking.

People might hold it together for a little while, but then they tend to panic.

You want to stop the flames from burning up your life savings and the solution seems obvious: pull out of the market. But what you don't realize is that this is essentially pouring gasoline on the fire.

Initially, you might feel better because you took action. You sold your stock and now at least the bleeding has stopped. But at some point (probably sooner than you think), the market will heat back up. Then you'll feel the pain of missing the opportunity to make your money back.

How often do you experience fear or anxiety about your financial situation?

Have you ever grimaced when looking at your account, seeing how your hard-earned nest egg is going down fast?

And how often do you experience greed? Admit it. At some point (be honest!) you've muttered to yourself, "Don't I deserve another zero at the end of my paycheck?"

We're never satisfied with how much money we have. No matter how many zeros there are, we always want more.

Whether you're just starting out or you've already amassed a healthy portfolio, you need to understand how fear and greed drive investment decisions. Too often, these emotions become the tail wagging the dog. Letting fear or greed be the force that drives your investment decisions will absolutely destroy your financial future.

It's not really a matter of "if," but "when." You may get lucky here and there, but sooner or later, you'll end up on the losing side.

If you're entering a commissions-driven marketing environment, investment professionals are keenly aware of how to play to both your fear and your greed. Which of the two emotions is in the spotlight depends on what part of the economic cycle we're in.

THE "FEAR" CYCLE

To quote hip-hop group A Tribe Called Quest, "Scared money don't make none."[2]

I once advised a group of investors with a complicated trust. It had a very down-the-middle allocation of 60% stocks in companies and 40% fixed-income instruments like bonds and money market funds, mostly comprised of index funds for the benefit of the beneficiaries. Everyone was in favor of this conservative approach, which was laid out in an investment policy statement.

Fast forward to the market meltdown in 2009. The entire world is losing money in an unprecedented way. When the allocations had been developed (and the markets were high), everybody fully bought into this down-the-middle approach. But with the markets in turmoil, some of the investors got scared.

Panic and fear spread throughout the group.

Despite objections, changes were made to the investment strategy and lots of money was lost.

Selling low was a very common occurrence at the end of 2008 and beginning of 2009. People were tired of watching their money disappear as the market tanked. They were scared that it would continue going in the same direction, so they felt the need to take action.

Of course, doing this meant they lost more than they would have if they hadn't done anything at all. While this is an illustration of how fear manipulates people into making decisions, people often overlook that "doing nothing" is also a decision. Oftentimes, it's the savviest one of all.

The majority of the time, staying the course and doing nothing is the best option.

As the market goes up, it's easy to feel optimistic, hunger for more, and take greater risks — because that optimism turns into overconfidence. When the market goes down, pessimism, fear, and regret ensue. Following the S&P 500 for a 10-year period until 2023, you can see the cycle of fear and greed mimicking the rise and fall of the market in the chart below.

INVESTOR PSYCHOLOGY CYCLE

When the market began to recover, people started to realize the gravity of their mistakes. It took several years for the investors I was advising to get back into their equity allocation. But zeroes were never recovered because they had sold at or near the bottom. That's the thing about fear. It increases as markets decline.

The irony of this is the greater the fall, the better the opportunity when the markets recover, but most people don't view it this way.

My goal with this chapter is to change this perspective. Investing requires discipline. It requires sticking to the plan and minimizing decisions. The huge mistake with the investors I advised (and most people during crises) is allowing fear to negate a well-established process.

THE "GREED" CYCLE

And then there's greed. In the 1990s, there was a kind of water-cooler game where investors would brag about how well their portfolio was doing and feign pity on those who suffered merely average yields. If your portfolio wasn't returning 5% to 10% better than growth stocks, you were a loser.

The mantra of the era was Gordon Gekko — played by Michael Douglas in Oliver Stone's *Wall Street* — stating with authority that "greed is good." Gekko's sentiment is often misunderstood, incidentally, because the full context of his speech has to do with shareholder inefficiencies and lame duck corporations. Gekko defines his motivation to clean up a badly-performing company as "greed." Today, we'd call that being an activist investor.

Fast forward to today, and crypto bros are famous for the same evangelical zeal.

It almost becomes an obsession, the new paradigm where growth is assumed and underlying value doesn't matter. This creates a herd mentality, where people almost blindly invest in something because others are and they don't want to miss out (remember that financial FOMO I talked about earlier?).

A striking example of the herd mentality was evident in the phenomenon of growth mutual funds in the late '90s.

While they were multiplying like rabbits, one firm, Janus, dominated.

In 1998, Janus' flagship fund was up 39%. By 1999, it was up 47%. A second fund, Janus Twenty, grew by 73% in 1998 and 65% in 1999.

According to published sources, by the year 2000, Janus was making as much as $1 billion per day.[3]

And then the tech bubble burst, sending that market into a freefall. Growth stocks gave back their gains ... and then some.

So, what happened to Janus?

Because it was deeply invested in tech and telecom companies like America Online, Cisco, and Microsoft, it was heavily exposed to the most vulnerable sectors. Janus held such enormous positions in tech that it wasn't able to get out as shares fell across the sector. In a two-year period, from 2000 to 2002, Janus dropped 64% and Janus Twenty lost 69%.[4]

Crypto speaks for itself. The 2022 Super Bowl might be best remembered for crypto ad after crypto ad. In an ad that both he and his agent probably now regret, Matt Damon looked everyone in the eye and shared the profound truth that "fortune favors the brave."

Yea, well. He was working for Crypto.com — hopefully paid in legal tender — and before the next Super Bowl, the company had carried out two major rounds of layoffs and its utility token, the CRO (and, no, I can't explain what that is) had "dropped by nearly 96% this [2022] year."[5] Whatever a CRO is or does, I don't think going down like that was the plan.

When your neighbor is making a bundle by flipping houses, investing in hot stocks, buying Bitcoin, or whatever the hottest thing may be, the feeling of missing out can inspire you to go out and do what they're doing. Like everyone who invested in crypto based on Super Bowl ad advice. As Matt said, fortune favors the brave!

And this isn't the first time this has happened. The 2000 Super Bowl was dubbed the "Dot-Com Super Bowl" due to all the tech ads, most infamously Pets.com.[6] That company, the hottest of the hot, raised $82.5 million in investment money the month after it dominated the Super Bowl ad wars with a singing sock puppet (really, go watch it on YouTube).[7]

Lots of people invested lots of money in Pets.com, which filed for bankruptcy well before the next Super Bowl.[8]

If you've done something like this, throwing money in the same direction everyone else was chucking it, thank your very human herd instinct. It can get you in trouble.

During market corrections, I have watched people concentrated in growth positions have very dishonest conversations with themselves. Here's how those conversations went, and still go today.

First, they say: "It's just a buying opportunity, I'm not worried." Next, they say: "Wow, this is painful but I still have gains and my funds will come back." Finally, they concede: "Oh my God! I'm bleeding! It's not going to stop until my gains are completely wiped out, and I'm forced to sell."

Adding insult to injury, this final revelation usually happens somewhere near the market bottom, making the investor's losses permanent when they bail.

Although your emotions may tell you otherwise, if you're switching strategies or buying financial products based on fear, greed, or really any emotion (or Super Bowl ad), then you're usually buying the wrong product at the wrong time.

Think about it. You're nervous because the market is already down, and you get greedy when the market is flying high. Too often, you'll end up buying the product you should have bought years ago or selling a position you should hold.

Fear and greed are extremely powerful emotions. Both push investors to act against their own best interests. I've seen very logical people become irrational when in the grips of either emotion.

I'd also argue that's EXACTLY how Wall Street likes it.

A Wall Street executive once told me he was in the "money-moving business ... the fear and greed business." We like to think of our investment advisers as people who look out for our well-being (like the ones in TV ads). And sometimes that's true but other times, the people you hire to advise you have the exact opposite goals. This means you need to be wary of them.

Stock transactions (whether you're buying or selling) generate fees and commissions. That's how financial firms make money — the more transactions there are, the more fees there are. If firms do nothing, commissions go down, revenue drops, and your money manager's salary decreases. But when they move money, they make money. That's just the way it is.

So, how do Wall Street firms motivate investors to keep trading so money managers can earn their fees?

They sell investors' advice that takes advantage of people's fear and greed. When the market is low, they might tell you to sell; when it's high, they might tell you to buy. The more you move money around, the better it is for your adviser. However, that's *not* necessarily what's best for you, the investor.

Pay close attention to the marketing messages Wall Street sends. They buy Super Bowl ads too. Take a more balanced approach, one that's not based on the extremes of fear and greed.

So, when do you sell?

If your portfolio is properly diversified and your goals haven't changed, the answer is ... drumroll please ... "never."

To give you an idea of how the stock market changed during and after the 2008-2009 recession, let's take a brief look at one index.

On October 9, 2007, the Dow hit 14,164.43 — the highest ever to that point.[9] Over the next 17 months, it bobbed up and down, finally landing at its lowest point of the downturn (6,594.44) on March 5, 2009.

People who sold their stocks during the recession were scared or desperate (sometimes both). Regardless, they missed a massive opportunity to make their money back ... and then some.

Ten years after the market first started to fall, the Dow closed at 22,775.39 on October 10, 2017 and continued to climb from there.

Unlike that wheel-and-deal image Wall Street sells, the reality is that most of the time, you don't need to sell. They want to sensationalize the investment process, hyping things with minute-by-minute ticks of market fluctuations. Watch CNBC for five minutes. There's so much going on! The reason for the drama is because investment firms are trying to sell you opportunity and drama.

Their goal is to heighten your fear and your greed with a purpose of making themselves more money.

But if you want a portfolio that performs at the highest possible rate over the course of your lifetime, it's going to feel like watching paint dry. It's going to be *incredibly* boring. You're not actually going to be doing much of anything. As long as you have a good process on the front-end, you actually have very little reason to talk to your financial adviser.

Keep a line from one of Sue Grafton's novels in mind: "... pretending to do something when you're doing nothing is an art form in itself."[10]

If you find yourself in a position of maximum fear, when the pain is too much to bear, then you made a wrong turn long ago. When the market is down, you've already experienced most of the declines, so selling at this point almost never makes sense. It usually does more harm than good.

FINDING AND MAINTAINING BALANCE

Maintaining a *diversified* portfolio smooths out your returns over time. The highs aren't so high, and the lows aren't so low. This process effectively keeps you in the game. A diverse portfolio also keeps you from falling into fear or irrational exuberance, both of which will lead you to make bad decisions. Remember that Wall Street is always happy to sell you something.

In that Super Bowl ad, Matt Damon was quoting the Latin phrase *audentes fortuna juvat*. Here's another one: *caveat emptor* ("let the buyer beware").

In order to let your portfolio grow the way it can (i.e., by leaving it alone), you have to come to terms with a few things:

You Might Do Something Stupid

You have to accept that it's possible (and probable) that you're going to do stupid stuff — and then learn how not to do the stupid stuff. For example, investors that made changes during the Great Recession lost a massive amount of money. And it was a natural, completely understandable moment when they were scared. But if they'd paused for a moment to look at the bigger picture and avoid the stupid stuff, they'd have been in a much better financial position before President Obama's first term ended.

Confirmation Bias Will Get You

You have to realize your own confirmation bias. When it rains day after day, you assume it will keep on raining, right? Well, that's not necessarily true, just like it's not true that if the market goes down one day it will continue to go down the day after that or the day after that. The same goes for the market going up. You must set this bias aside and realize that the stock market is a marathon, not a sprint. You're in this for the long haul, not just to make a quick buck.

Your Emotions Are Not an Indicator

Finally, you need to get a grip on your emotions. Confirmation bias, on the days the market is down, is going to play into your fears and tempt you to sell. Remember, selling at the bottom isn't going to do you any good. The market will go up and it will go down. We know this. The best way to capitalize on the money you've been pouring into your asset bucket is to stick with investments long-term.

GO SIMPLE AND JUST LEAVE IT ALONE

My business partner and I have taught this philosophy in many different economic environments, to both small and large investors.

When we started in 1998, people would argue with us. They had heard the news, the marketing, and the hot stock tips. Previous versions of the Pets.com sock puppet and Matt Damon had spoken to them.

Our approach was too measured for them. And we asked why they would spend the time and money on the class and not listen to what we had to say?

Then we asked who was better off: the investor who earned a steady 5% return every year or the investor who earned a 50% return one year, but lost 50% the next?

Heads were scratched and assumptions examined.

So, what's the solution? Almost always, the answer is a mix of low-cost stocks and bonds invested in low-cost index funds.

Which you then leave alone.

The disciplined growth investor must never put too much of their allocation in growth stocks. They know that even though it feels good during market highs, it feels far worse when the portfolio gets killed.

You're in an environment that is actively working against you.

You have to work really hard to harness those fearful and greedy emotions so you don't make a hasty mistake that costs you.

It's all about balance and patience.

Possessing great resources creates great risk of being pitched "exclusive" investment opportunities. This tends to cause successful individuals to pursue complicated strategies with a high rate of failure or underperformance (looking at you, crypto).

A "boring" portfolio of stocks, ETFs, mutual funds, and real estate doesn't often have the appeal of riskier investments — but that's the appeal. That portfolio is the more prudent choice for building and preserving wealth.

LESSONS AT A GLANCE

- Don't make decisions out of fear or greed.
- Markets can go up slowly and crash down quickly.
- When you have a balanced portfolio, you will own things that are doing well and things that aren't.
- Don't buy more of what is doing well while selling what isn't. Do the opposite. Better yet, don't do anything.

- Fear is normal in down markets.
- When making a decision to sell or buy out of fear or greed, you need to make two decisions: when to sell *and* when to buy. Continually making such decisions is almost always a loser's game.

CHAPTER 6
HOW TO TURN $100 MILLION INTO NOTHING

"Remember that leverage can never turn a bad investment into a good one, but it can turn a good investment into a bad one (by forcing you to sell at just the wrong point in time)."

– James Montier

How does a successful businessman go from bringing home $100 million to ending up in debt?

This is the story of the rise and fall of an old friend of mine. Let's say his name is Jack and he owned a successful chain of stores across Arizona, about 20 in all. He was wildly successful. But as his business thrived, he made two major mistakes.

First, his lifestyle kept pace with his income.

The more he made, the more he spent. By this point in the book, you know that he should have been filling up his asset bucket. It's probably not a surprise to learn that he wasn't doing that.

His second mistake was expanding his empire outside his knowledge base.

Think Elon Musk jumping from manufacturing to social media. Way different business.

Jack was very knowledgeable about one particular industry, which is why he was so successful within it. But he chose to venture into a different area entirely by opening a restaurant, and if you've ever tried to run a restaurant, you know it's a very complicated business. It seemed like a good, safe deal but Jack didn't understand it. He strayed from his core competency, chasing a bright, shiny object into uncharted territory.

At some point, Jack had a friend who told him about an "amazing" opportunity to head up this restaurant deal (when you're wealthy, there is always a friend or a friend of a friend ready to tell you about the next best deal). But in order to finance the deal, he had to take on a vast amount of leverage.

Leverage is just another way of saying debt — it's how much business owners borrow against the value of their business.

Many business owners use debt as a way to grow their business in a reasonable way, such as opening additional locations or expanding a product line. However, many businesses fail because they take on *too* much debt.

Basically, live by the sword, die by the sword.

Debt in and of itself isn't necessarily a bad thing. For a business it is, and should be viewed as, a tool. Like a surgeon's scalpel, its effectiveness lies in how it's used. Keep in mind that the same is true for personal debt.

I've already mentioned the dubious transaction that Elon Musk dove into by buying Twitter. How'd he finance it? By leveraging Tesla stock (and no, Tesla's other stock owners were not consulted on this, which is a whole other can of worms)[1] and causing the stock to fall by 65% on the day he purchased it (October 17, 2022). More than one thing was affecting the value of Tesla stocks, but Twitter wasn't helping.[2]

With that in mind, back to my friend Jack. He increased his leverage by borrowing a lot of money to cover this major purchase. He was convinced there was no downside or risk. But of course, there was risk. There is *always* risk.

Just as Jack and his business partners bought the restaurant, the real estate market cratered. And what happens when people suffer economically? They cut back on unnecessary expenses. They don't go out to eat as much, which meant revenue from his "real job" started dropping.

Previously, the cost of running his business was manageable, since there wasn't a big debt anvil attached to it. But his new debt, and the added expense that came with it, meant his overall business costs quickly became untenable.

My friend Jack's business suffered horribly.

The restaurant folded. Eventually, he had to sell his successful business to pay for his losses (like Musk has had to sell Tesla stock to support Twitter[3]). In the end, my friend lost everything including his marriage, which fell apart from the stress of his financial collapse.

In his quest to establish multiple streams of income, Jack made a common mistake: He took a huge risk on *one* opportunity in an area outside of his expertise. The restaurant deal demanded too much leverage from him with too big of a learning curve. Even if the market hadn't crashed, it would have been, at best, a shaky investment. Jack made a classic mistake: A person's own internal optimism and belief in how smart they think they are (even if they are very smart) is a recipe for winning a losing bet with risky investments.

Having a second or third income stream does you no good if you have to invest all of your first one to access it.

I cannot stress this enough. New investments need to be carefully calculated and should *never* put your existing stream(s) of income in jeopardy.

Elon Musk has gargantuan existing streams of income, yet he still got himself into a pickle.

Remember, you don't have Elon Musk money. Thus, you don't have his margin of error.

HOW THE RICH USE CREDIT

According to the Federal Reserve Bank of New York, Americans had nearly $1 trillion in credit card debt at the beginning of 2022.[4] While the average American consumer may carry the hefty weight of credit card debt, the ultra-rich view credit as just another tool in their investing toolbox.

A 2014 Bank of America survey of high net worth individuals found that the wealthy are very strategic about how they use credit. High net worth individuals used credit "… to invest opportunistically, buy real estate, pay taxes, fund education expenses, and start a new business."[5]

For example, when interest rates are low, it may make sense to take out loans even if you could afford to pay cash. Even though he could have chosen to pay for it outright, Facebook CEO and billionaire Mark Zuckerberg chose to carry a mortgage on his $6 million home. The idea behind this is that if money can provide a higher return through investing, it works more wisely when parked in your portfolio.[6]

Of course, this is contingent upon securing a mortgage with an interest rate lower than what your returns are.

It's just math.

Similarly, when creditors offer less than 1% interest rates, tapping those lines of credit to pay taxes is basically like getting a free loan. So, even if you have money available to pay for something outright, it may be in your best interest to use debt to finance an investment, whether it's a new business venture or a new property.

The key distinction between how the wealthy use debt versus how the poor use it is that the rich don't use credit to finance their lifestyle. They know how much to take on, how much to pay back, and how interest rates should work toward — not against — their bottom line. Any leverage they take on will be for the purpose of investing in assets that pay off continually, rather than depreciating in value over time (like cars and yachts).

This isn't overly complicated.

Instead, it's viewed as rational, non-emotional decision-making.

The wealthy will only take on as much debt as makes sense mathematically. In the example above, Jack started on this path but was overly optimistic about risk. His mindset was that of the poor.

Blinded by the opportunity laid out before him, he was unable to see that his actions were putting his entire future at risk.

When the real estate market crashed, it wiped out his entire financial structure, including his personal fortune.

When it comes to personal credit cards, the ultra-rich also have a drastically different take compared to the ultra-poor. *Rich Habits* author Tom Corley found that wealthy people used fewer credit cards, but when they did, they paid their monthly balances in full (and on time) and used perks to their advantage.[7]

By contrast, the poor did pretty much the opposite, including maxing out all their lines of credit.

It can be simplified this way:

- Good debt returns money to you at the end of month.
- Bad debt takes money from you at the end of the month.
- Good debt is part of an overall financial structure that has money working for you.
- Bad debt is an ongoing cost that doesn't contribute to your current, or future, finances.

When surveying any investment opportunity, consider the kind of debt you're taking on — even if the word leverage is used — and whether it will return money to you.

Is it an investment or a liability?

Don't make decisions that cost you money.

THE $25 MILLION WINDFALL

I met Debbie in 2009. She was fresh out of a divorce settlement that left her with a house and $25 million in assets. Her ex-husband is a Silicon Valley executive and, as part of the settlement, she received several million in a tech stocks.

Although she enjoyed an affluent lifestyle while married, once the divorce was finalized she had to learn how to manage her millions more or less overnight.

In that way, it was not unlike winning the lottery.

As discussed before, there are two ways you can think about money:

- What can my money buy?
- What can my money support?

Debbie was like so many who come into sudden wealth — she focused on what $25 million could buy.

She immediately donated some money to charity. She bought a 50% share in an incredibly expensive vacation house. She began building her family a newer, bigger home. And because she was so asset rich, she decided to build this new home while still living in the home she already owned. She took on debt to finance both.

Like everyone else who's ever built a house, Debbie faced unexpected construction costs as the project took longer than anticipated. The original budget ballooned. She was also hit hard by the 2008 economic downturn. Her portfolio, including her tech shares, dropped significantly. The value of her vacation home, and both of her other homes, plummeted.

Debbie still had $12 million, but that was down significantly from $25 million.

And because of her spending, even that was not enough to support her family and pay off her debts. She was forced to sell her dream home for $2 million less than she believed it was worth. She sold her vacation home at a loss, and her family moved into a more appropriate home (given her new and not improved level of assets).

Following debt payments, Debbie went from $25 million in assets to $12 million to $8 million.

Debbie's situation illustrates the key differences between the ultra-poor and the ultra-rich. The smart move is to always be a pessimist.

The ultra-poor are not pessimists. They're the most optimistic people in the world.

Here's what Debbie should have done. Since a $25 million bank account supports a lifestyle of $1.2 million annually before taxes, all decisions — like gauging the affordability of a new home — should, therefore, be looked at through the lens of $1.2 million. This makes spending decisions much easier.

Debbie's $1.2 million lifestyle should have been structured with no debt payments and a fixed cost of living at $150,000, including budgeting for private schools and other large expenses. The amount leftover would then be reserved for discretionary spending.

Keeping fixed costs low and discretionary spending high provides a family with tremendous flexibility when a down-market cycle hits.

You can easily rein in discretionary spending. But changing fixed costs is impossible without selling assets, usually at the wrong time in the overall economic cycle. If Debbie had focused on living off $1.2 million instead of $25 million, she would have made much better decisions.

THE OTHER SIDE OF SPENDING AND LEVERAGE

Lou Grubb was something of a legend in the Phoenix area, known for his folksy commercials touting his local car dealerships. Meeting Lou remains one of the highlights of my career. He fully embodied the ultra-rich lifestyle, from the way he ran his dealerships to the way he managed his life.

Lou moved to Phoenix in 1945. A few years later, he landed a job as a junior salesman at a Ford dealership. In 1972, he was presented with the opportunity to buy it. Given his frugal spending strategy, he was the only one of his peers that had the savings to do so. That meant he wasn't on the wrong side of leveraging.

Grubb's initial purchase turned into a car dealership conglomerate that he would later sell to AutoNation in 1997 for a fortune. He was so popular and well-known that in 1977, Arizona Republicans courted him to run for governor, which he declined, preferring to focus on his business. He died in 2012 at the age of 89.

The most important detail here is that the initial opportunity to purchase the dealership was not just offered to Lou. It was also offered to his fellow managers.

Lou could've had at least one business partner in that deal, potentially even two or three. But because Lou had lived frugally for so long, he was the only employee to have built up enough savings that could be activated when the time came.

Luck isn't happenstance. Luck is made. As Lou's story shows, what passes for luck is actually the result of preparation.

Instead of spending himself into a bigger lifestyle, Lou Grubb saved a lot of money. Then he could make a business deal that wasn't overly leveraged.

He carried no personal or business debt. He taught his family about money management and kept his investments simple. Lastly, he gave back to his community.

Perhaps we could all grow to be ultra-rich if we learn to adopt Lou's philosophies.

WATCHING DEBT AND CASH FLOW

The key issue to keeping debt in check is understanding its relationship with the rest of your financial life.

Typically, you'll have fixed expenses, like rent and utilities, that don't vary too greatly. That total cost is important because it dictates the minimum amount of money you need to earn each month. Additionally, you'll have variable expenses such as food and clothing. These fixed and variable costs combined give you your monthly household costs.

Any money you have left after paying household costs is your free cash flow.

That's what you should be investing. Reviewing how much (or how little) free cash flow you have after paying bills gives you an honest assessment of whether or not you're overspending.

If you have a portfolio, you should be looking into whether or not it is generating enough income to handle your lifestyle expenditures. If Debbie had reviewed her portfolio before taking on big expenses, she would have clearly seen she was overspending. Her negative cash flow ate into her principle.

Another extremely useful financial tool is to track the last five years of your income versus spending.

This provides insight into how your lifestyle reacts to increases in income. It's not always an easy answer, as a five-year span may include rising unavoidable and necessary expenses, such as child-care or medical bills. And, of course, it's important to analyze what's needed versus what's desired. Also, make note of any debt you took on that increased your overall spending.

Whether or not you're blessed with sudden wealth or you've built your wealth slowly over the better part of a decade, your portfolio must keep meeting its obligations. It needs to grow so it generates enough money to replace your income.

As we discussed previously, letting emotion get into the decision-making mix leaves you open to far more risk. Your ration can fly out the window.

Focus on using debt sparingly or strategically, not merely as a way to accumulate *stuff*.

Too much debt, as we've seen, can prolong the time before your portfolio works for you, as opposed to the other way around.

Your main goal is to build a consistent, stable relationship between leverage and spending. One that can sustain you for the rest of your life. You can't do that if you're overspending and misusing debt.

LESSONS AT A GLANCE

- Focus on what money can support rather than what it can buy.
- Leverage of 75% to 100% is inherently risky.
- Make a concerted effort to quickly pay down personal debt.
- To prepare for market downturns, save one to three years of cash to cover expenses.
- Stay disciplined with your spending. Keep leverage low.
- Keep fixed expenses low.

CHAPTER 7
PROCESS VS. STRATEGY: HOW NOT TO GET SCREWED

"If you stop at general math, you're only going to make general math money."

– Snoop Dogg

So much financial advice is focused on, and based around, the tick-by-tick movement of the markets. People obsess over it. Everyone is searching for the next move. The next opportunity. And when you experience sudden wealth, it's easy to wonder how you can turn your new lump sum into more. But, proceed with caution.

At every turn, news producers talk up any event — no matter how insignificant in the real-world — and bring in experts (as if they really have a clue as to what's going to happen next). It might make for entertaining television, but it's a complete waste of time.

Think about all the so-called experts that make predictions about what the market will do.

They're rarely right. And if they are, it's not likely they'll be right again anytime soon. The market call they made probably had a lot more to do with luck than actual skill.

For example, Jim Cramer, host of CNBC's aptly named *Mad Money*, has made a career of basically yelling about investment opportunities (among other things). But his track record is far from great.

In fact, one research team came up with the "inverse Jim Cramer strategy" that basically explored how they would have done if they just did the opposite of what Cramer recommended:

> This approach was successful in generating … a one-year return of 20.13%, as compared to the S&P500 which generated a negative 6.29% return […] While often the target of criticism for his slightly lackluster stock-picking performance, the *Mad Money* host is without a doubt one of the most influential TV personalities in the history of finance TV. However, it remains a given that his stock-picking abilities seem to have slowly deteriorated over the years. When indexing his stock picks weighted by the frequency of his on-air buy recommendations, they seem to, on average, produce what

are far from excellent year-to-date results, often underperforming the market.[1]

As I mentioned in a previous chapter, a senior adviser once told me we weren't in the investment business; we were in the "money-moving" business. Essentially, that term emphasizes that when you move money, you make money — at least if you're a broker.

I'll say it again: Moving money isn't always what's best for you. In fact, most of the time it's a poor decision for the investor.

Let's take a look at the slow-rolling scandal that has embroiled Wells Fargo over the last decade. It makes it pretty obvious that investors, at least the nonattentive ones, do not hold the best cards at the investing table.

Since first surfacing in 2013, fraudulent activity in Wells Fargo's sales department has led to additional government fines as more and more dubious activities have been uncovered. These include opening fraudulent customer accounts and other dishonest sales-driven activities.[2]

> "The fact that a large institution of such importance was nevertheless able to engage in fraud and effectively illegal transactions on such a scale — that is staggering," Cornell Law School professor Saule T. Omarova told CNBC.[3]

There are plenty of ways for your advisers to make a lot of money off of your money. They can intentionally push products that come with higher fees or some sort of kickback (such as commissions or bonuses).

In Wells Fargo's case, advisers were instructed to "funnel clients with assets of more than $2 million into a higher-fee platform known as Investment Fiduciary Services,"[4] which produced a windfall of extra money in annual fees.

To make matters worse, fee structures of various investment products are often difficult to figure out. Many advisers and banks (including Wells Fargo) claim their fees are transparent. However, that's not often the perception of investors. People have a very hard time understanding what their annual fees are and why they exist.

They simply don't know what percentage they pay to their adviser. If you have one, do you?

This lack of knowledge is not *entirely* the investor's fault. What makes this difficult is the many layers of fees and how they're deducted. Many of them are named in such a way that they sound perfectly legitimate, so the investor doesn't ask questions. Others are technically billed to you but are still auto-deducted from your account, so they don't need your permission or approval. It's kind of the same con that medical billing uses: flood the zone and hope a lot goes unnoticed (or is simply misunderstood).

The other key issue is that commissions and fees vary greatly depending on the product type. These range from annual fees between 0.5% and 1.5% to commissions from 1% to 7%. So, given the amount of money you put in an investment, the compensation for the adviser is disproportionate. If they can make 5% to 7% off one product, why would they sell you a different one that will make them less money?

It's a massive conflict of interest.

Take a moment to ask yourself:

- Would you buy a car without knowing what the interest rate was?
- Would you purchase land if no one told you what you'd be paying in property taxes?

I have to believe you wouldn't. Both would be terrible decisions. So why are you willing to sign onto something your investment adviser is selling if you don't fully understand the terms?

It's time to learn more. In order for this process to work, you need to be able to trust the person you're giving your money to. As Ronald Reagan so famously said (he borrowed the line from a Russian proverb) "trust, but verify."

Step one is to find a certified fiduciary adviser.

This is someone who must put *your* interests above his or her own when making financial decisions for you. They must present you with investment vehicles and products that will best advance your needs and goals — and not just those that make them the most money.

This may seem like a no-brainer. Shouldn't your investment adviser work for *you?* You hired them, right? The bottom line is that they aren't legally required to put your interests first, unless they're a certified fiduciary.

The environment of the investing world, where everyone's goal is to make money, is not built for *you* to actually make money.

It's built so your advisers, and their bosses, make money.

This pressure to maximize profits is an aspect of the ongoing saga of Wells Fargo:

> Experts said the government has wide authority to limit
> Wells Fargo, given the reputation senior management has
> earned for imposing demanding business goals on its work-
> force. These lofty goals may have led employees to engage in
> deceitful and, at times, allegedly illegal behavior.[5]

The majority of financial advisers are not going to be on your side (again, they aren't legally required to be), so you have to know what you're doing before you ask someone for help. You're going to have to watch your own back because they're not going to do it for you.

The service Wells Fargo "provided" to customers whose assets were worth at least $2 million was called Investment Fiduciary Services. Even the name they chose is misleading since a fiduciary adviser must legally put his or her clients' best interests before their own. But the very nature of this practice (putting clients with higher levels of wealth into a higher-fee platform) ignores what's in the best interest of the client. And, in all fairness, for some clients this platform may have been the best but it certainly wasn't for every high-asset client.

It's practices like these that make it so important to make sure the financial or investment adviser you're hiring is a certified fiduciary. It's *crucial* you ask the person you're considering to hire about his or her credentials because not all advisers have adopted this standard. Some claim the fiduciary standard will reduce the variety of products they can offer their clients or limit the advice they can offer.

I'll be blunt: neither of those things is true.

They don't want to be fiduciaries because it reduces the amount they can earn in commissions and fees.

So, if you don't see this standard in writing, make sure you ask if they're certified fiduciaries.

And then make sure you get it in writing.

There are three very critical ways you can protect yourself:

- Hire a certified fiduciary adviser.

- Have a defined investment process in place.
- Put **EVERYTHING** in writing: the return you're aiming for, the amount of risk you're willing to take on, and the total fees you're expected to pay.

Most investors end up with a return *below* the market average. Generally, this is because people panic and sell when they should hold tight (and other silly mistakes). Regardless, most people don't have a defined process for how they make investment decisions. The data speaks for itself — the following chart from Dalbar, shows that during a 20-year period (1995-2015), the market outearned the average investor.

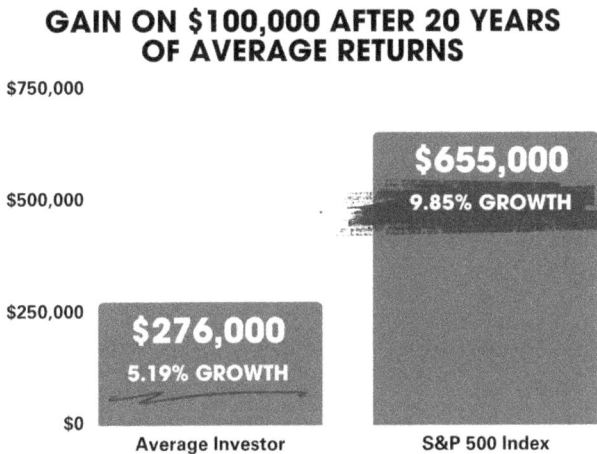

GAIN ON $100,000 AFTER 20 YEARS OF AVERAGE RETURNS

$750,000

$500,000

$655,000
9.85% GROWTH

$250,000

$276,000
5.19% GROWTH

$0

Average Investor   S&P 500 Index

GOAL-SETTING

Setting goals is about figuring out what you want to do and what the time frame is. Your ability to grow (or deplete) your sudden wealth starts with this.

I want you to focus on the answers to three questions (I suggest grabbing a pen and paper, or your phone, to make note of these):

- What do I want to do?
- What can I do?
- How can I prioritize?

When facing these simple questions, people often realize their short-term objectives are at odds with their long-term goals. You might want, and think you can afford, the fancy sports car *right now*, but you have to weigh material (and even charitable) desires with the long-term needs of yourself and your family.

Like Dolly's mama said, "Always keep something back for you." That Maserati won't do you any good in 40 years when you can't spend time traveling because you're broke again.

It's often hard to think that far into the future, but the ultra-rich investment process actually starts with an analysis of what you're doing today. What does your lifestyle look like? What would you do differently if you had more time ... if you could do anything at all? How would your priorities change?

Wealth is not measured by how much money you make but by how much money you keep.

Financial freedom is when passive income meets or exceeds earned income.

This is when opportunities open up and you can make choices that were previously out of reach.

I'll use one of my former students as an example. At the time he took my class, Ned was working for a successful company in Silicon Valley and making a nice salary with stock options, but he didn't really like his job. He was married with two kids and felt a bit stuck in his job at that point. It may not have been what he wanted, but it was stable and being the millionaire-next-door-type, he lived on far less than he made, which allowed him to put away more than half of his annual income.

A couple of years later, the company was acquired by a tech giant. All of a sudden, his stock options were worth a hell of a lot more.

While the idea of staying with the company was certainly an enticing one, especially with the possibility of the stock value increasing, what he really wanted to do was get involved in the startup world. He wanted to be more creative and have more freedom to explore his passions. But of course, startups can't pay what more established companies can, which made him nervous — and understandably so.

It's very hard to walk away from a six-figure salary and stock options that seem to be skyrocketing.

We discussed his options, priorities, and passions. The acquisition could go one of two ways: It could explode and his stock options would be worth millions, allowing him to retire early or go into the startup world more comfortably, *or* the whole thing could go bust and he'd lose the majority of his money.

In his situation, those stock options would come in handy. They opened doors for him.

I posed the following scenario. If he were to sell his stock and diversify his portfolio, he'd have a substantial stockpile of cash. He could take a job at a startup for a smaller salary, plus a healthy amount of stock options (which is pretty typical with startups) and still feel like he was doing right by his family. He'd have his investment portfolio to fall back on in the event that the startup crashed and burned. He could pursue his passion, as opposed to following the short-term swells in stock, which would provide far more fulfillment than staying in his old job.

Even with this option on the table — one in which he got to pursue what he loved and still be financially stable — Ned balked. He wasn't sure he could take that leap and suggested working for another two years before venturing into the startup world, a classic example of chasing money rather than dreams. For most people, this might seem like a good compromise. You get in a couple more years, let your stock value climb, and stash more money away.

The trouble with this is that you probably aren't going to leave after two years. You'll get to that two-year mark and you'll be even more comfortable than you are right now. If your stock value grew, you'll wonder how much more it could grow. You'll want to stockpile more money.

Maybe you had another kid in the meantime or bought a bigger house. Suddenly, you think another two years will do it. Then in the blink of any eye, 10 years later, you're still having the same conversation.

What's interesting about this scenario is that it poses an intriguing dilemma.

Ned could stay at his current job with a handsome salary (even though it's unfulfilling) or sell his stock, leave the company, and pursue his passion — *with financial stability*.

In other words, he could stay in his comfort zone, or he could try something new. It's not hard to figure out which is the safer option.

The struggle people face revolves around the uncertainty.

Ned had a stable gig and choosing to take a job at a startup is intrinsically scary. We're afraid of what we don't know. And there was no way for Ned to know if he was making the right call by quitting his job. However, there was plenty of evidence telling him it was a bad idea, most of it coming from within his own mind.

Ultimately, Ned chose to forgo future opportunities (his old job's growing stock) for today's priorities (exploring something he enjoys while being financially stable), which is exactly what you should be doing. He left the company, sold his stock, and ventured into the startup world. Ned did what many people are afraid to do, or don't know how to do: Pursued his passion when he had enough money rather than staying the course, unhappily, to see where it goes.

The end goal — not the potential opportunity — should be the driver of your decisions.

This is why goal-setting is such an important part of the investment process. You *must* determine the most important goals in your life, in their proper order, before you can proceed through the steps to reach them.

Ned never could have come to his decision without putting his priorities in order.

BUILDING YOUR ALLOCATION: AVOIDING PANIC

Now that you've written down your goals and prioritized them, the key is to craft an investment allocation that generates a rate of return (RoR) that will accomplish your goals at a level of risk, or volatility, that you're comfortable with.

You need to mix in enough safe assets with the riskier, higher-reward assets. The exact ratio will depend on your overall desired level of risk.

The most important thing you need to learn about allocations is that the focus should be on the long-term strategy, not the short-term play. So many investors make decisions with the short-term in mind.

They get scared because the stock market goes down or because one particular part of their portfolio is declining. They panic.

Investment allocations consist of two parts — expected return and volatility — in two different classes.

The next chart shows the variance in annual returns for various stock and bond portfolios from the years 1926 to 2016, according to Vanguard. Understanding how these two classes behave differently (and then mixing the right amounts of them as portfolio ingredients) is the basis for this discussion.

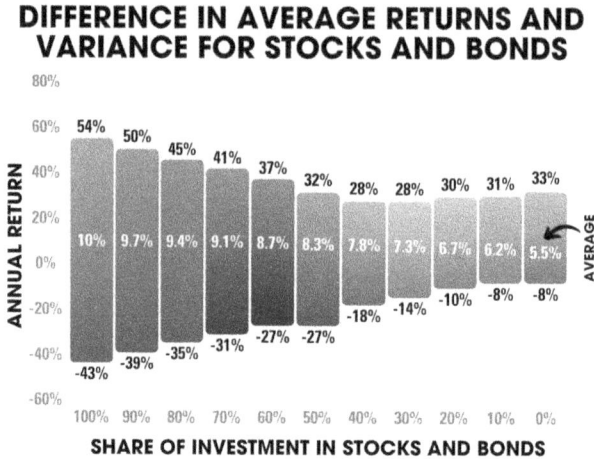

DIFFERENCE IN AVERAGE RETURNS AND VARIANCE FOR STOCKS AND BONDS

Share of Investment	Annual Return (high)	Average	Annual Return (low)
100%	54%	10%	-43%
90%	50%	9.7%	-39%
80%	45%	9.4%	-35%
70%	41%	9.1%	-31%
60%	37%	8.7%	-27%
50%	32%	8.3%	-27%
40%	28%	7.8%	-18%
30%	28%	7.3%	-14%
20%	30%	6.7%	-10%
10%	31%	6.2%	-8%
0%	33%	5.5%	-8%

SHARE OF INVESTMENT IN STOCKS AND BONDS

Equity

Equity assets include owning stock. When you buy stock, you own a piece of the company. It comes with a higher rate of return, but also has greater risk. Bigger companies tend to be more stable, but don't have the same growth opportunities that small companies do, so the long-term rate of return is lower.

Stocks are further divided into many different subsets: large versus small, value versus growth, domestic versus international, and real estate. The biggest factor in your portfolio is the percentage you have in equities. The second biggest factor (though it has a much smaller impact) is the type of equity you own.

Always remember that the higher the potential return, the greater the risk you're assuming.

And while those high returns might seem appealing, it's not wise to throw all your money into a high-risk pot.

You need to reserve some of your portfolio for lower-risk options, even if it means a smaller return. We're striving to keep the ride smooth, not to fly into turbulence at every opportunity.

When one stock group is up, another might be down. But you'll barely notice because you've diversified. Instead of seeing the line moving steadily up or in freefall, you'll see a gentle curve if your mix is balanced.

Fixed

Fixed assets include bonds issued by the government (federal, state, and local) or corporations. Bonds are basically just loans. When you buy bonds, you're loaning an entity some money and they'll pay you back with interest (albeit, a small amount of interest).

Because governments and large corporations generally have pretty good credit, they're very likely to pay you back, which means you're assuming a low amount of risk — but also a small return.

Some argue that, in the long run, the risk associated with bonds isn't as low as it appears because you're surrendering purchasing power. The money you're tying up is actually decreasing in value due to inflation. This then becomes a conversation about how many stable, low-return investments you need to mix in with short-term, volatile, high-return investments.

As with stocks, there are many different types of bonds that will help diversify your portfolio. But again, all of them typically have a low rate of return.

Risk Diversification

Generally, I recommend keeping your bond risk low and having most of your risk be in equity investments.

This allows for risk diversification while maintaining a level of security.

When we discuss this in my class, students tend to have a lot of questions, the most common being: *If stocks have the best return, why not invest 100% into them?*

The answer is simple. During a bad market cycle, stocks can go down as much as 50%. Heck, it doesn't even have to be a bad cycle. Things happen, like Tesla stock dropping about 65% after Elon Musk bought Twitter.[6]

This slices your wealth in half. To further complicate matters, stocks don't go back up very fast during a market recovery. Historically, they *do* recover, but if you've lost nearly everything, watching those numbers slowly climb is going to be painful.

Most investors don't have the stomach for this type of movement. So, they add safer assets to their portfolio to smooth things out during downturns. Of course, by doing so, they also reduce the expected return.

This is why investment advisers recommend owning asset groups that behave differently.

In order to smooth out the ride, you need assets that don't go up and down in tandem. Regardless of what stocks you own, when the market is down, all stocks generally go down.

However, as demonstrated by the following chart, which reflects data from Morningstar, Inc. and Hulbert Ratings, stocks and bonds typically don't move in the same direction at the same time.

STOCKS AND BONDS RARELY MOVE TOGETHER

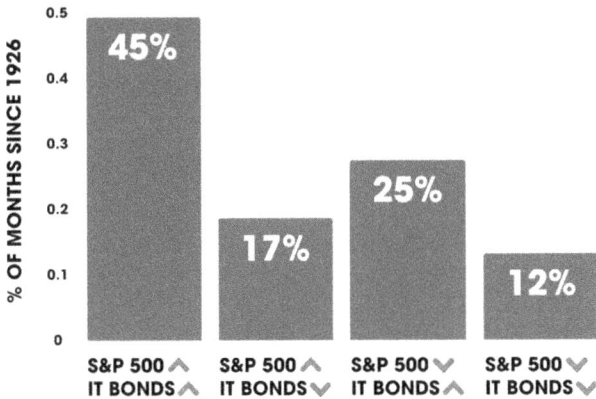

Furthermore, the longer you hold an asset, the higher your chances of hitting the long-term average — and your risk will continue to diminish over time. Similarly, the longer you hold stocks, regardless of economic events, the closer you get to the long-term average.

The next chart, based on 2022 data from JP Morgan Asset Management, represents the range of outcomes you can expect in any given year. Look what happens over the long-term after five, 10, or 20 years. The allocation still has the same average return, but the worst-case scenario is significantly better.

Investors get obsessed with short-term results, then make long-term adjustments because of stock-value swings, regardless of favorable or unfavorable performance metrics.

I call this the investing head fake.

COMPARISON OF STOCK AND BOND RETURNS OVER 64 YEARS

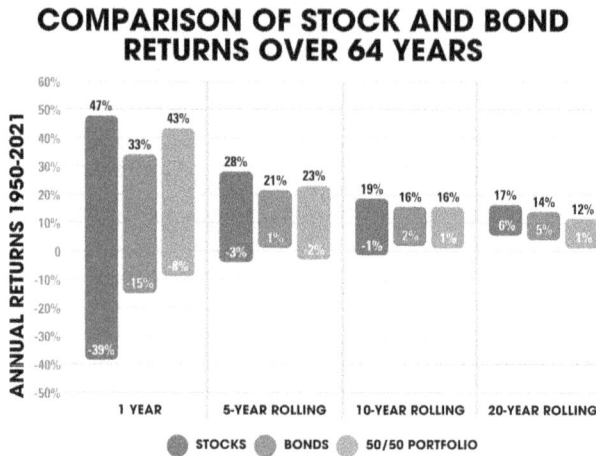

PASSIVE OR ACTIVE APPROACH?

The passive versus active discussion centers around two different philosophies:

- The *passive approach* says markets are efficient. This philosophy is based on the assumption that current prices reflect all known information and that time is on your side. Leaving your investments alone is the best way to capitalize on your returns.
- The *active theory* suggests a skilled manager can beat typical market returns by capturing otherwise unnoticed opportunities or dodging risks.

I go into much further detail on this step in Chapter 8, so I'm not going to elaborate too much here but at its core, the answer is simple and effective.

The bottom line is that finding the right active manager is difficult. If you do find one, you may also find that they charge much higher fees than you're interested in paying.

As you've probably guessed, I'm completely in favor of the passive approach. It's not that active managers *can't* beat the markets — it's that they rarely do. If professional managers can't seem to do it very often, the average investor isn't likely to do any better.

Time and time again, I've seen clients think they can do better than the index funds I recommend, then we watch them lose huge sums of money.

If you think I'm wrong on my passive approach, read the upcoming section about Warren Buffett's decade-long bet pitting low-cost index funds against high-cost hedge funds. If a passive investment is good enough for a *billionaire*, the fifth richest dude in the world as this is written,[7] it should be good enough for everyone.

Stick with index funds. Period.

MONITORING AND REBALANCING

Without a doubt, this is the most important aspect of the investment process, yet it's the one most people seem to neglect. Strong monitoring and control systems are crucial to achieving the goals you set at the beginning of this chapter. Without them, you're asking for trouble.

Rebalancing involves adjusting your allocation according to the goals you've set and not letting your fear or greed override those plans. Keep it simple and remove as many decisions as you can by setting parameters beforehand.

Remember, what can't be measured can't be managed. The quarterly performance reports your adviser provides should make it easy to track the following:

- Performance relative to your goals.
- Performance relative to the market and your benchmarks.

- Performance relative to risk.
- Performance relative to target allocation (rebalancing).
- Personal spending.

You should review these reports diligently, but don't let a down quarter take your eyes off the prize. There's a difference between being responsibly informed and allowing your fear to take over.

Think of monitoring like using a compass. You're never *really* on course in the middle of the ocean or flying a plane. You're always slightly off-course and making incremental adjustments so you point in the direction that will take you to your destination.

If you don't have a compass, then you can start flying south and not notice the wind is blowing you off course. You'd have no idea until you see mountains instead of ocean. By then, small changes won't get you back on course.

Monitoring is simple:

- What did you make?
- What did you spend?
- What did you save?

WRITE AN INVESTMENT POLICY STATEMENT

An investment policy statement (IPS) is a written document that provides both you and your investment adviser with a concrete set of goals you'd like to achieve. It details exactly how you plan to achieve them.

Here, you can outline specific allocation instructions, the level of risk you're comfortable with, and just how liquid you'd like your assets to be.

In addition, an IPS is a good place to lay out processes for monitoring your portfolio (such as frequency and type of report) and the circumstances under which you'll permit a change in allocation, liquidity, or passive income.

And remember: *Everything* you do with your financial adviser should be in writing. Doing so protects you as much as it protects the adviser. Our memories are fallible and we shouldn't rely on them in matters that carry such high stakes. It's too easy for you to remember something differently than your adviser does.

If it's all in writing, there's no room for misunderstanding.

For example, let's say your IPS states that your No. 1 goal is to retire at age 60 with enough saved that you and your spouse can travel frequently and live comfortably. Beyond that, you'd like to have a moderate inheritance set aside for each of your children.

These goals should each be outlined (and prioritized) in your IPS, along with the steps you're comfortable taking to get there and the timeframe for each.

I cannot stress the importance of having your investment strategy in writing enough. It doesn't have to be super complicated, but it needs to ensure that you have sound processes in place.

This document will be something that keeps both you and your adviser on the same proverbial page. It will also possibly stop one of you from deviating too far from long-term goals in favor of short-term, riskier propositions.

As much as none of us like to think about how easily we can be taken advantage of, this isn't an area where you want to test the waters.

Ask anyone who had their "virtual" assets parked at FTX Trading Ltd., the crypto exchange that basically lost $8 billion in 2022 under the guidance of Sam Bankman-Fried, a guy who put the "bro" in techno bro (he liked to play video games during business meetings and once wore shorts and a T-shirt onstage with Bill Clinton and Tony Blair).

He has quickly become his generation's symbol of financial malfeasance, joining his forebears Bernie Madoff, Ivan Boesky, Elizabeth Holmes, and the granddaddy of them all, Charles Ponzi:

> In a letter to staff obtained by *Bloomberg*, Bankman-Fried apologized to employees and explained that FTX's collateral (the assets a debtor will seize if the borrower can't pay back their loan) decreased from $60 billion to just $9 billion. While Bankman-Fried didn't break down which of FTX's assets make up that collateral, *CoinDesk*'s initial report indicates that Alameda used $2.16 billion worth of FTX's FTT token as collateral when taking loans out … Let's not forget about that wave of "unauthorized" transactions that robbed FTX of an additional $477 million (that the thief continues to launder). We still don't know who's behind the theft, but some skeptics believe it was an employee on the inside of FTX.[8]

Think you're too smart to get taken like this? The divorce lawyers of Tom Brady and Gisele Bundchen probably bought new boats just dealing with how much the former couple lost in the FTX collapse. This was after they starred, while still happily married, in one of those 2022 Super Bowl ads (Brady owned 1.14 million shares of FTX, while Bundchen owned 686,761).[9]

The busier we are, the more likely we are to miss the signs, and the more time passes, the more likely we are to let our guards down. Every relationship is like that, even the one you have with your investment adviser. Maybe you have a few good years with them and you stop reading the quarterly reports. Maybe the report didn't even come last quarter and you didn't notice.

Here's another example from the world of sports. In the first weeks of 2023, news broke that Usain Bolt, one of the greatest sprinters of all time and an eight-time Olympic gold medalist, had discovered "… that more than $12.7 million [was] missing from his account with a private investment firm in Jamaica." According to Bolt's lawyer "the Olympic champion's account once had $12.8 million but now reflects a balance of only $12,000."[10]

For every bankrupt celebrity, there's a financial adviser being sued. And I'm not saying it's always completely the adviser's fault (it almost always has to do with overspending and lack of control, as we've discussed in previous chapters). But with an IPS, there are processes in place to prevent such things. And if an investor *does* run into financial trouble, the IPS is the beginning of the paper trail to prove it was the adviser's fault (or, on the other side of the coin, it's where the adviser can start to prove he or she *wasn't* at fault).

Both in business and life, we rely on relationships. But when it comes to your financial stability, you *need* to rely on written policies.

Your IPS can help protect you from letting emotion (whether fear, greed, or pressure from existing relationships in your life) cloud your judgment and lead to investment strategy changes that will work against your goals. Time invested in writing this policy will be time well invested.

Again, Leave It Alone

The final step is the secret to success: leave everything alone. Follow the process. Remember, keep it simple. The less you mess with it, the better off you'll be.

Practice saying the word NO.

Every time someone comes to you with a "great idea" or the "next big thing," politely decline and move on with your day.

One of the FTX Super Bowl commercials that Tom Brady and Gisele Bundchen starred in went like this: They both look at their phones — obviously the process by which all important financial decisions are made — and Tom says, "I'm in." Then they call a bunch of "normal" people and lean on them to get "in."[11]

This is how you lose money. When Gisele and Tom (well, maybe not in tandem anymore) call, just say "no." Don't listen to the Giseles and Toms of the world.

You have a process down and it doesn't involve investing in your brother-in-law's startup or with some guy who never grew out of his Epsilon Theta frat lifestyle.[12] It *does*, however, involve making fewer decisions, and I'll make this one for you.

Stick to your plan. Don't deviate. Even when people are trying to butter you up.

It's not the products and opportunities you pass up that will create problems. Often, it's what you *do* buy (but don't understand) that gets you into trouble.

You really think Tom Brady ended up with 1.14 million of (now worthless) FTX stock because he understood cryptocurrency and blockchain like he did an NFL playbook?

And, most importantly, make sure you focus on your goals.

They should dictate every investment decision you make, which should be few and far between anyway because you're leaving things alone.

LESSONS AT A GLANCE

- Simplify your process.
- Have a clear vision about your goals. Prioritize them.
- Say no to all "opportunities" people try to sell you that aren't already a part of your process.
- Eliminate decisions. They're not helping you.
- Stay the course. Make adjustments to your allocations, but only when necessary.
- Keep it simple.
- Keep your adviser fees low (under 1%).
- Low turnover is crucial. Again, make fewer decisions.
- Create easy monitoring systems.
- Put everything in writing.
- Did I mention keep it simple?

CHAPTER 8
MAKING FEWER DECISIONS: THE PASSIVE APPROACH

"Simple can be harder than complex: You have to work hard to get your thinking clean to make it simple."

– Steve Jobs

Ask anyone what a typical day on Wall Street or in the investment sector looks like and they'll conjure up images from movies like *Boiler Room*, *Wall Street*, and *The Wolf of Wall Street* or TV shows like Showtime's *Billions* and HBO's *Industry*. All feature a romanticized vision of financial experts and deal-making.

In films and TV, the star trader is always searching for new information, placing calls at precisely the right moment, and staring at a fast-paced ticker of code that flashes by. He is (and the trader is usually a he) making multiple decisions at all times, and even working through complicated math equations in his head. It's like the investor version of *Everything Everywhere All at Once*. Oh, he's also usually a dysfunctional human being.

And so, it follows that the average investor is primed to think that he too can (and should) make as many decisions as these fictional characters. It's not hard to fall for the romantic notion that, with a little bit of research, you can be like *Billions* hero Bobby Axelrod, seeing angles elusive to everyone else in the game.

What if I told you that when it comes to financial investing, you should do exactly the opposite of what you see on TV?

Remember that research team that gamed out doing the exact opposite of what Jim Cramer recommended and ended up doing better?

The fact is, the more decisions you make, the more likely you're gonna make a wrong one — maybe *the* wrong one.

WHAT THE NUMBERS SHOW

Every year, investment research firm Dalbar releases its Quantitative Analysis of Investor Behavior, which tracks how individual investors and investment managers perform relative to various market benchmarks over time.[1]

Here are some of the key findings for the year-end 2015 report:

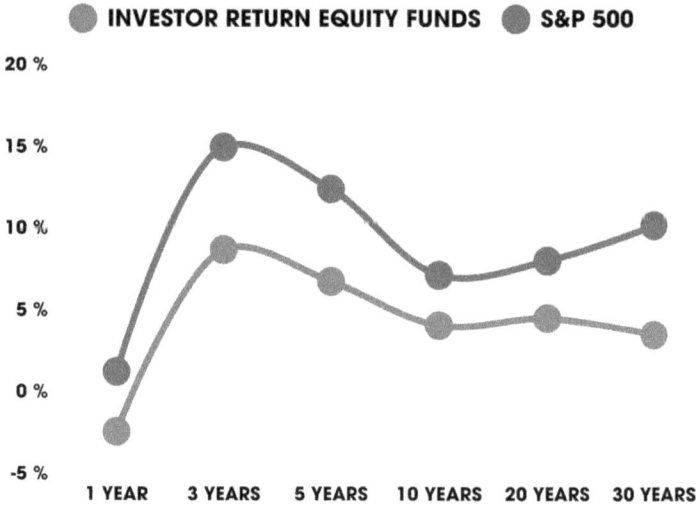

INVESTOR RETURN EQUITY FUNDS ● **S&P 500**

The total return rate is determined by calculating the investor return dollars as a percentage of the net of the sales, redemptions, and exchanges for each period. Based on investor returns versus the returns of the S&P 500, it's easy to see that placing your bets on individual investment decisions, rather than going with the indexes, can end up costing you about 2% to 6% in returns.

Just one year of such "lost" returns can be tough. But consider what the end result would be of losing out on an additional 2% to 6% every year over two decades.

Such losses occur for two primary reasons:

- **An active versus passive approach:** Some investors stick with long-term index funds, while others depend on active managers — who are paid a lot of money — to anticipate where the market is going and take action to earn the most money. Remember, transactions are where money managers make their money.

- **Changing mutual funds:** Investors make changes to their plan (either to allocations or specific mutual funds) at the wrong time, either out of fear or greed. Fear takes over when the market is down and greed rears its head when the market (or a specific stock) is going up.

Let's examine these two pieces and how they affect both decisions and returns in further detail.

Beat the Market: Active Versus Passive Decision-making

As I take a hard look back on my career, I have to admit that the accounts that performed best over the long-term were the ones that required the least amount of investment decision-making by me.

This leads to a controversial subject that continues to rage among investment professionals and investors: Can you ever outperform the market?

Every single decision an investor makes actually masks two perspectives.

What do you buy? And when do you sell?

When these two questions get run through the gauntlet of fear and greed, you're bound to fail.

A story in *The Wall Street Journal* on this subject caught my eye a few years ago. It was about how, in early 2007, legendary investor Warren Buffett bet the asset management firm Protégé Partners $1 million that an S&P 500 index fund would outperform its hedge funds over a 10-year period.[2] If the funds outperformed, Buffett would donate $1 million to charity. If they underperformed, Protégé Partners would donate the $1 million.

Would you have taken that bet?

I should note that 2007 created a particularly advantageous environment for the hedge funds since they're designed to protect investments during down years.

Now would you have taken that bet?

Well, according to Buffett:

> I made the bet for two reasons: (1) to leverage my outlay of $318,250 into a disproportionately larger sum that — if things turned out as I expected — would be distributed in early 2018 to Girls Inc. of Omaha; and (2) to publicize my conviction that my pick — a virtually cost-free investment in an unmanaged S&P 500 index fund — would, over time, deliver better results than those achieved by most investment professionals, however well-regarded and incentivized those "helpers" maybe.[3]

Before we go further, let's explain a "fund of funds." Most investors can't, or won't, buy a single hedge fund because such an investment is entirely too risky. A fund of funds is just a basket of managed hedge funds that smooth out risk.

Buffett bet against such a basket, which contained somewhere between 100 and 200 actual hedge funds, and won pretty substantially. Buffet's regular old S&P 500 index fund earned an annual average of 8.5% during the 10-year period (a final gain of 125.8%). By contrast, the highest performing fund of funds returned an average of 6.5% (with a final gain of 87.7%), while the lowest-performing fund of funds turned a mere 0.3% average (with a final gain of just 2.8%).

The bet concluded on December 31, 2017. The annual return of the hedge funds was just 2.2% while the S&P 500 index fund was 7.1%.

This differential is not small by any means. Over 10 years, a 2.2% annual return is a cumulative 24.3% increase, while the annual 7.1% return is a 98.6% increase. As an investor, the difference between nearly doubling your money over 10 years (98.6% return) versus only a 24.3% increase is staggering.

Buffett's bet against Protégé Partners is the perfect illustration of active versus passive investing.

Passive investing means letting your money mirror whatever happens in the broader markets that it is invested in.

Whether that's the Dow Jones, the S&P 500, or international stocks, passive investment is a basket of stocks that will mimic the market very closely. When the market goes down, your portfolio goes down. When the market goes up, your portfolio goes up. That's it.

Active investing is the opposite strategy, an attempt to outsmart the market with brilliantly researched, perfectly timed buying and selling.

The argument for active investing is that skilled managers consistently boost returns over and above the market. They make claims like, "If the market rises 10%, I think we can do 12%." However, what's not in the brochure is that often the active manager will net around 6% of that.

Buffet's passive approach returned three times what the active managers made.

This is especially troubling for the fund of funds because the performance period included the worst economic cycle since the Great Depression, a period during which one might have expected hedge funds to strongly outperform the market.

The Myth of the "Best and the Brightest"

We all want to believe our financial professionals are clever, that their firms are well-informed, and that they understand how to navigate the markets in a way that will prevent us from ever losing money. We want so desperately to believe this, but is it true?

A 24-hour news cycle of "experts" on CNBC, Bloomberg TV, and Fox Business provides a wealth of opinions. Jim Cramer's show, *Mad Money*, includes a "Buy, Sell, Hold" segment where he tells a riveted audience about what he thinks is going to happen and, of course, which stocks should be bought, sold, or held. And thus was born the "inverse Jim Cramer strategy."

We hope if we listen to enough industry "experts," we'll learn how to keep our money safe — or better yet, make more money.

It's the same reason people spend two hours on Sunday mornings watching fantasy football shows. People like to think that if they can learn just a little bit more and soak up just a fraction of someone else's expertise, they'll become better investors, fantasy football players, gamblers, or whatever. And yet, people forget that the house almost always wins — it's why casinos and gambling websites turn a profit.

The advice we hear speaks more to our apprehensions than to our assets.

The investment world is a treacherous and volatile landscape, which is why investors go to advisers in the first place. They hope the adviser will protect them if things go wrong.

If that's true, then it makes sense to pay the advisers to help your portfolio stay away from the shoals during rough economic seas.

However, it's not true.

The harsh reality is that most advisers simply can't say what will happen in the future. Just look at the investment banks during the 2008-2009 financial crisis. They ended up going hat in hand to the federal government for bailouts.

The simple truth is that the majority of index funds will consistently beat any active manager.

For the last 20 years, the overwhelming majority of actively managed public equity funds failed to match the performance of market indexes over time. According to the S&P Indices Versus Active (SPIVA) 2022 U.S. Scorecard, published by S&P Dow Jones Indices, 96.85% of active domestic funds underperformed their respective benchmarks over a 20-year period from Jan. 1, 2003 to Dec. 31, 2022.[4]

In October 2016, *The Wall Street Journal* published a multipart series on this topic dubbed "The Passivists."[5] It explored the passive investing trend, which was called "one of the largest migrations of money in history"[6] and its impact on the financial world:

> Over the three years, ending Aug. 31, [2016], investors added nearly $1.3 trillion to passive mutual funds and their brethren — passive exchange-traded funds — while draining more than a quarter trillion from active funds, according to Morningstar, Inc.[7]

While not exactly declaring that the art of stock picking was dead, the Journal certainly made the case that passive investing is here to stay, and that when the data for both styles of investing are compared, passive investing consistently makes better financial sense than trying to guess where the market is headed next.

The following chart outlines this, showing the percentage of U.S. equity funds that failed to beat the benchmark index during three time periods: five, 10 and 15 years preceding 2022, according to the SPIVA 2022 U.S. Scorecard.[8]

PERCENTAGE OF U.S. EQUITY FUNDS OUTPERFORMED BY BENCHMARK

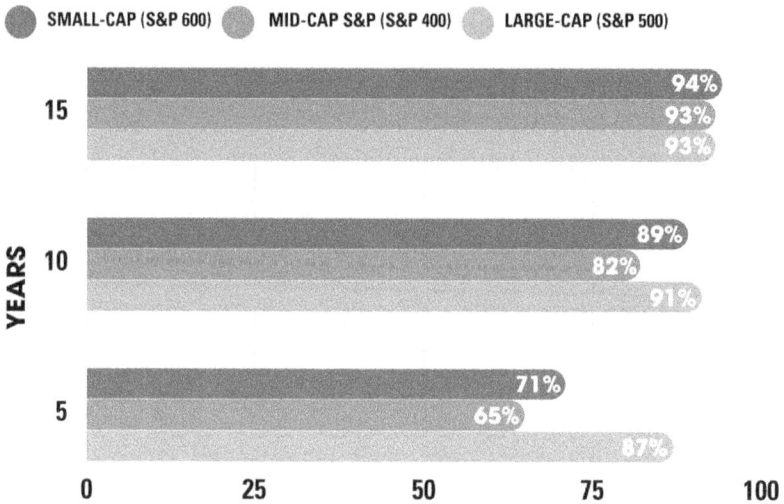

● SMALL-CAP (S&P 600)   ● MID-CAP S&P (S&P 400)   ○ LARGE-CAP (S&P 500)

YEARS	SMALL-CAP	MID-CAP	LARGE-CAP
15	94%	93%	93%
10	89%	82%	91%
5	71%	65%	87%

0   25   50   75   100

Why Decision Fatigue Matters

Before we get to more investing examples, let's consider a common scenario: choosing a new paint color for a room in your home.

Let's say you've already narrowed down the choices from all the possible colors in the spectrum to basic white.

But upon arriving at the paint section of your local hardware store, you're confronted with a wide array of elaborately named colors that are all variations of white. There is eggshell and ivory and off-white and cream and snow and something called buttercream. There are whites with yellow undertones and whites with blue highlights. There are apparently very few things that are merely "white."

Scientists have started to study what exactly happens in the brain as you make decisions, when you slowly narrow all those whites down to just a few shades and then to the one that goes in the paint can.

It's called "decision fatigue."[9] Every time you are forced to make a decision, your brain has less energy to devote to considering the next decision. For example, as it gets later in the day you're more likely to indulge in quick (and bad) decision-making, like going with the double cheeseburger and extra-large fries that wouldn't have seemed wise earlier in the day.[10]

This is not to be confused with the "paradox of choice," which involves being given so many options that people become paralyzed and opt-out of choosing altogether.

Rather, decision fatigue has to do with the cognitive impact of actively making decision after decision after decision.

In the case of paint, after carefully considering the first 30 whites, by the time you get down to the last three shades you're more likely to just pick one at random and call it a day. Or you may spend hours agonizing over 30 different shades of white, and then give up when the time comes to find a complementary shade of blue for the hallway. Too many choices are just one of the factors that can influence decision-making.

Another unnoticed variable is food. Indeed, how hungry you are later in the day also sways decision-making. This phenomenon has been noted in a study of parole decisions by judges.

Several years ago, researchers examined more than 1,100 judicial rulings that took place over a 10-month period. All of these rulings were made by a parole board judge who was essentially determining whether or not to allow criminals to be released from prison or, in some cases, allow a change in their parole terms.

While you may think the judges' decisions were primarily influenced by factors such as the type of crime committed or their behavior in prison, that isn't necessarily the case. Researchers found that parole decisions were influenced by factors that shouldn't have an effect in the courtroom at all, such as the time of day.

At the beginning of the day, a judge was more apt to give the person a favorable ruling (roughly 65% of the time). However, as the morning wore on, and the judge became more drained, the likelihood of someone getting a favorable ruling steadily dropped, all the way down to zero in some instances.

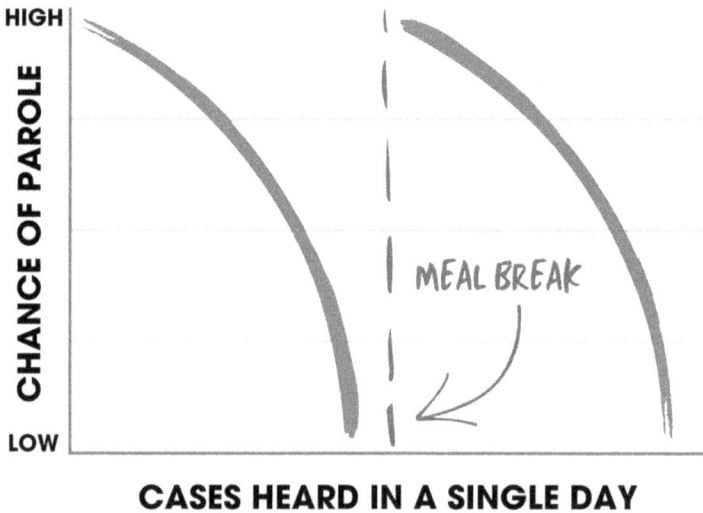

CASES HEARD IN A SINGLE DAY

But following a lunch break, a judge returned to the courtroom somewhat refreshed, and in turn, the probability of a favorable ruling went back up — only to drop back down again as the end of the day drew near. This trend occurred regardless of whether the crime was theft, embezzlement, or murder.[11]

Similarly, in the case of investing, you may start out wanting to make very careful decisions. But as those decisions pile up, you start to cut corners or not give each decision your fullest attention. This phenomenon becomes even more prevalent if you're making a series of decisions all at once, such as when markets are volatile and you're feeling pressured and are trying to weigh several choices before the closing (or opening) Wall Street bell.

Warren Buffett: The Oracle of Omaha

Consider Warren Buffett and how he missed the dot-com boom.[12] Many investors misunderstand his underperformance during the late 1990s. By the conclusion of 1999, Buffett's stock performance was down 50% while the rest of the market soared.[13]

Many investors jumped ship when they felt Buffett had lost his touch. But what actually happened is pretty simple: Investors confused an underperforming asset category with a badly performing asset manager.

This goes back to piling on more decisions rather than laying low. Would you fire Warren Buffett when he's not doing well? If so, who replaces him? Are you not just selling low and buying high?

When investors run, they look at whatever parts of the market that are doing well.

What happened when the dot-com boom imploded and the Nasdaq collapsed? Buffett's performance started to look real good:

> Buffett suffered a 49% loss from June 1998 to March 2000. At the same time, the Nasdaq rose 140% and the S&P 500 rose 28%. Despite heavy losses and public ridicule, Buffett stuck to his guns and wouldn't touch internet stocks. Buffett's ability to stay disciplined might be more admirable than his analytical skill.

At the time, I'm sure people were wondering if Buffett had lost his golden touch or if he would ever outperform the market again. A near 50% loss for a stocks investor during the biggest bull market in history doesn't inspire confidence. But he had the last laugh after the bubble burst, gaining 80% over the next two years while the Nasdaq lost 72% and the S&P 500 lost 28%.[14]

As I've stated before, in times of turmoil — and even during booms — the smart move is to do nothing at all.

PREVAILING IN A SALES ENVIRONMENT

When you decide to take an active investing approach, you're buying into the "sales environment" of investment firms and advisers who brag about how they're the ones — part of what *The Wall Street Journal* once called "the winning 15" — who can outperform the markets.[15]

But consider the other side of the equation. On the passive side is Buffett, who won that bet against Protégé Partners and didn't lose his shirt during the dot-com crash.

When you're actively managing your account, you have a lot of decisions to make:

- Do I buy equities?
- Should I invest in small-cap or large-cap funds?
- Is Russia going to invade Ukraine?
- What's happening with the economy?
- Do I buy commodities? Which ones?
- Do I hold gold?
- What should I do when interest rates change?
- Is Ukraine going to defeat Russia?
- Should I be on the offense or the defense?
- When do I sell?

Think about the risk of decision fatigue outlined earlier in this chapter. I'd argue that investors are not immune from it and are therefore not equipped to make investing decisions on the fly.

Not only are they untrained, but there's an emotional element at play. How confident are you that you'll make the right investment decisions at the right time, every time? And if you can't do it, are you really confident your active account manager can?

Buffett certainly isn't convinced. Here are his thoughts about the ability of everyday people to guide their own financial futures:

> It is not necessary to do extraordinary things to get extraordinary results ... By periodically investing in an index fund, the know-nothing investor can actually outperform most investment professionals.[16]

Buffet, and others, believe we are creating problems for ourselves by playing along with the financial adviser game.

In my classes, where I try to help people regain control of their finances, I use the great book *Winning the Loser's Game: Timeless Strategies for Successful Investing*. Its author, Charles Ellis, puts it this way: "A lot of times investing is a loser's game. People try to win, and by trying to win, they lose."[17]

I tell those in my classes: "Here's a strategy that over a 10-year period is going to overperform; it's going to win 90% of the time." Frankly, most of them would be foolish to do anything else.

But, in essence, that's what many do.

Buffett knows a whole lot of good money managers. He has contacts with every good firm.

Yet he candidly tells us he would put his money into index funds rather than trust the more active money managers with his funds.

Likewise, when asked how he would instruct the trustees of his estate about investing the proceeds of it, Buffett's advice couldn't have been simpler:

Put 10% of the cash in short-term government bonds and 90% in a very low-cost S&P 500 index fund. (I suggest Vanguard's.) I believe the trust's long-term results from this policy will be superior to those attained by most investors — whether pension funds, institutions or individuals — who employ high-fee managers.[18]

Buffett realizes that the issue is not just the active versus passive approach, but that when active managers are brought into the equation, another variable that is not present with index funds is also introduced: you.

Investors can (and often do) panic. That's when they fire their current manager and get a "better" one; however, this decision usually has adverse results.

As history shows, managers generally can't time the market to improve returns, so your decision to change managers will likely cost you money.

If you're not yet convinced about holding on to a long-term approach, here's one more example.

Bruce Berkowitz was Morningstar's manager of the decade ending in 2007. Money poured into this fund at a staggering pace, but then the banking crisis hit.

As the market went into turmoil, Berkowitz went from "really smart" to "really stupid" in the eyes of many investors. They had bought into his fund based on his long-term record, but they sold based on a short-term market downturn.

Berkowitz wasn't any smarter or dumber in either environment. In one scenario he had the wind to his back, and in the other he was sailing into a hurricane. Yet investor funds poured in and out at exactly the wrong time. This is why there is so much nuance to the active versus passive discussion.

Hopefully the experiences of others can guide you. As the data cited earlier shows, with passive investing you're likely to beat active managers a majority of the time. It's a low-cost strategy because you have to do less, the fee structures are lower, and, because there's less turnover, it's more tax-efficient.

What Costs Less: How to Justify Fees

So, the question is, why would investors pay for active management when it actually produces lower returns?

There's not really a good answer to that question.

Because they are set to mimic overall stock market performance, index funds will incur fewer fees than active accounts that require research and more transactions to beat the market.

According to a March 2022 study by the Investment Company Institute, 25% of actively managed domestic equity funds have an expense ratio less than .77% compared with .17% for index domestic equity funds.[19]

Now let's consider the case of Nevada, where they always roll the dice, right?

A memorable 2016 front-page story in *The Wall Street Journal* described the typical workday of the man in charge of Nevada's Public Employees' Retirement System:

> Steve Edmundson has no co-workers, rarely takes meetings, and often eats leftovers at his desk. With that dynamic workday, the investment chief for the Nevada Public Employees' Retirement System is out-earning pension funds that have hundreds on staff. His daily trading strategy: Do as little as possible, usually nothing.

The Nevada system's stocks and bonds are all in low-cost funds that mimic indexes. Mr. Edmundson may make one change to the portfolio a year.[20]

What's key about Nevada's $35 billion fund manager is not just that he's increased the portfolio. It's that he's managed to save millions in costs with this passive approach. The story notes:

> If Nevada consumed a typical Wall Street diet, it would pay roughly $120 million in annual fees. In 2016, Nevada paid $18 million.[21]

While you may not accumulate a comparable $35 billion, all those fees do add up. And when something is cheaper — and more likely to be successful — why wouldn't you do that?

The State of Nevada. It takes your money … and keeps its own!

Fewer Decisions, Higher Returns

Employing a passive strategy means mirroring the market. That's all you need to do. You've made one decision that's low-cost and tax-efficient. That's your strategy.

The active guys are juggling five to seven knives while the passive guys are juggling one, very slowly. Which juggler is more likely to cut himself — and ultimately, you?

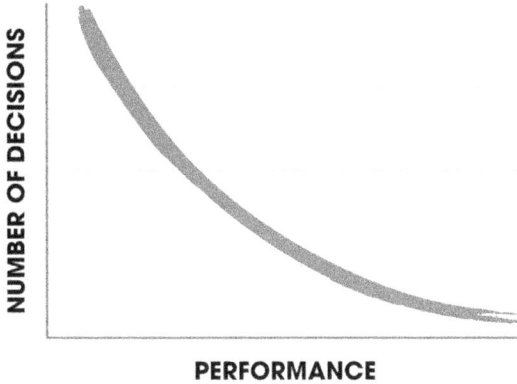

In light of these facts, should investors just settle for a passive approach to investment?

Hell yes!

Don't get me wrong. It's not that active managers *can't* beat the index. They can, sometimes they even do. It's just that finding the active manager smart enough, intuitive enough, and brave enough to do so is very difficult and time-consuming. And how much money will you lose trying out different active managers?

Investors should stick to index funds and stay the course, even when it doesn't appear to be working. This approach minimizes decision-making.

Making fewer decisions is the bedrock of portfolio management. Every decision you make provides a risky opportunity to introduce emotion into the equation. The fear you feel when the market dips can make you do stupid things. Ditto for the greed you experience when the market is going up.

Boring? Yes.

Effective? Absolutely.

This is true for the vast majority of people, including the one and only Warren Buffett.

This is one of the major secrets to being ultra-rich.

Those who are able to achieve high levels of wealth have an amazing amount of discipline during times of market upheaval. They stay the course, recognize that downturns happen, and understand the hazards of abandoning long-term strategies. They cut costs by skipping the expensive active managers. They get lean and eliminate decisions. Then they sit back and flourish.

To become ultra-rich, you have to learn the discipline of passive investing and stick to it.

LESSONS AT A GLANCE

- Minimize decisions — they fatigue you.
- Stick with low-cost index funds.
- Avoid active managers.
- Don't let short-term market dips change your strategy.
- Focus on the long-term.

CHAPTER 9
MISERABLE MILLIONAIRE OR ENLIGHTENED BILLIONAIRE

"Money can't buy happiness, but it can make you awfully comfortable while you're being miserable."

– Clare Boothe Luce

The goal of this book is to grow your sudden wealth and help you understand that risks are ever-present, but many times avoidable with the right mindset. Money, if well-managed and kept in perspective, can buy you happiness, or at least provide greater opportunity to find it. But it also seems to make some people miserable — or gives them more ways to make it obvious that they're miserable.

Having lots of money is no guarantee of anything. I've met many millionaires, and a few billionaires, over the years. Many of them were completely miserable. On the outside, they seem to have it all, but after you spend some time with them, you realize they're actually quite unhappy. The way they treat others is usually one of the first giveaways.

They're rude to people, especially those deemed "beneath" them. They're dismissive of the ideas of others. They're arrogant. They spend a ton of money on expensive possessions. Image is everything to them.

They're the type of people who only talk about themselves and how great they're doing when you run into them at an event. They typically surround themselves with people who are just like them. Their life is one big, self-centered quest to see how much of life they can consume.

Money does not change people; it just shows who they really are.

From an early age, we're taught implicitly that money — and everything that comes with it — is the universal benchmark of success. You get the money, you get the girl, you live happily ever after.

As Jerry Maguire is made to shout: "Show me the money!"[1]

But after getting the things that are supposed to add up to a successful life, many people end up wondering why the happiness they were promised did not follow. They desperately search for the missing piece, thinking maybe they don't have enough money, or maybe they picked the wrong spouse.

As David Byrne of the Talking Heads sings: "And you may find yourself in a beautiful house, with a beautiful wife / And you may ask yourself, 'Well, how did I get here?'"[2]

For many, the assumption that follows is that if another million is earned or someone else is married, then happiness will happen.

Wrong again. The cycle continues.

Talking Heads again: "Same as it ever was, same as it ever was."

These miserable millionaires all seem to share similar personality traits and habits that contribute to their gloomy outlook on life. And let's face it, you don't have to be a millionaire to be this way.

First of all, they're rarely happy — regardless of how much power they have, how much money they make, or how their status in society changes. The obsession with themselves and the quest for more (money, power, whatever) drives nearly every decision.

I mean, does Elon Musk seem all that happy running Twitter?

He regularly chooses to explain himself in tweets to someone with the handle @catturd2[3] and occasionally bans journalists from the site in a huff.[4] He decides not to pay the rent and fires the custodial staff.[5] As I mentioned before, he also lost a jaw-dropping amount of money — $182 billion just in 2022.[6]

They're dictators but, of course, they'd never see it this way.

This type of person has a very difficult time taking personal responsibility for his or her unhappiness. They consistently blame others for their problems. They're rarely at fault for anything. They believe that if others would just fall in line and do what they're told, things would work much better.

Since Musk bought Twitter, advertisers have fled. Savvy CEOs don't want their brand anywhere near Twitter as white nationalists, Russian bots, and crackpots inundate the space. They have no way of knowing just what their advertising is going to end up next to on screen.

But does Musk look in the mirror? No. He tweets:

> Twitter has had a massive drop in revenue, due to activist groups pressuring advertisers, even though nothing has changed with content moderation and we did everything we could to appease the activists. Extremely messed up! They're trying to destroy free speech in America.[7]

The miserable millionaires (and billionaires) believe external events will finally bring them happiness. They think that more money, a promotion, or a new toy will finally fill the void. For the most part, they're irritable and discontent with their lives.

There's a 12-step program for nearly every addiction, and they all begin with a central theme that is vital to long-term recovery: You must put down the addiction.

Then, you need to recenter yourself.

Instead of being an individual focused on him or herself, a person needs to focus on others. How can you improve someone else's life?

Self-reliance seems to make sense, but after years of interviewing and studying wealthy people, I can assure you the above issues apply. Meaning, if money is the drug and the person's sole pursuit is accumulating wealth, then it's a disease that will not bring the person true happiness.

If the team consists of me, myself, and I, the fruits of its collective labor will provide limited long-term joy, regardless of any "successes." Eventually, they get to a place in their lives where they realize they were supposed to feel fulfilled but aren't (or are denying it).

They've gotten everything they'd ever wanted, yet they felt empty.

This is a harsh realization that can leave anyone desperate.

This chapter stems from countless interviews that revealed the relationship between happiness and money. Much like drugs, money only provides a temporary fix to a much deeper problem. People that search for happiness through external means rarely find what they're looking for (cue up the U2 song).[8] Even if financial rewards come their way, they don't produce the desired result. True, long-lasting happiness comes from within.

With drugs, it's often easier to see that someone is masking their pain. With money, not so much. Wealth conveys a degree of success in our culture. Houses, cars, and nice vacations are all taken to communicate: "I have made it and I'm pretty pleased with myself."

However, if the pursuit is just the acquisition of stuff, it probably won't ever make you happy.

Many people believe that money solves problems — and to some extent, it does. You might not have to worry about paying your bills or feeding your children. But money doesn't fix what's broken on the inside. The bottom line is that the need and desire for more of whatever — money, drugs, fame, sex, etc. — is just a vicious cycle that can leave you forever unfulfilled.

You might be wondering if you're falling into this money trap. It boils down to one thing: People with money issues tend to focus on themselves and what they don't have.

So, how do you know if this is you? Let's check in with ourselves for a moment regarding miserable millionaire traits (that just about anyone can have):

- You never feel like you have enough. No matter what you buy, there's always something bigger or more expensive you "need." There's something missing and maybe you've spent a lot of money trying to find it.
- You tend to be overbearing, trying to intimidate people into compliance. It's your way or the highway.
- Nothing is ever your fault. Others (spouse, kids, employees, those damn "activist groups") need to change their mindset or behaviors — not you.
- The main thing that drives you is self-centered fear, like losing something or not getting what you want.
- If you own a company, your employees fear you and don't respect you. They come to work to get a paycheck but that's it. They don't buy into your vision because the bad stuff all rolls downhill. They're not loyal to you because you're not loyal to them.
- Your relationships with others are shallow. They rarely run deeper than the latest news, sports, weather, or business deal.
- People hang out with you not because of who you are but because of what you have.
- If you're married, it isn't going all that well, even though you might think it's fine (your spouse may have a different opinion). You may rationalize that away because you're a great provider.
- Your kids may have a different view of your family dynamics than you do as well.
- If you're married, perhaps you've had an affair or two.

The Miles Bron character that Edward Norton plays in *Glass Onion: A Knives Out Mystery* kind of covers the bases.

The good news? There's a solution.

TURNING THINGS AROUND

First and foremost, stop focusing on yourself and refocus on the people around you. Make it a priority to enhance other people's lives.

Take Dolly's advice: "Don't get so busy making a living that you forget to make a life."[9]

Start with your spouse, kids, and employees/coworkers. Make them look good instead of taking all the credit. Help them improve their skills. Work on their strengths and help them with their weaknesses.

Let others be the hero of the story, whether that's your family or your business.

Next, stop focusing on money. Focus instead on relationships and experiences. Listen more, talk less. Work on your own defects, rather than worrying about everyone else's.

If there's a problem, take ownership of it. When something goes wrong, accept that you're at fault. Hell, sometimes say that even when it's not true, just to take the heat off of someone else. See what you can do to fix it. Do things that make you uncomfortable. Ask for help. Give away a portion of what you make.

Remember, the people that matter don't want your money. They want your time.

I can also say another thing with certainty: Those that follow this philosophy actually tend to have a higher net worth than those who don't.

Why? They tend not to take huge risks with their money to prove something to everyone. They don't buy a bunch of expensive things they don't need.

Why am I talking about this? Because I used to be that guy. Nobody in my life had the courage to tell me what an asshole I had become (though I might not have listened even if they tried). So, instead, I learned the hard way.

Elon Musk is the richest person in world, though he did dip to the No. 2 spot for a bit. Therefore, nobody tells him he's being an asshole (though his ex, Grimes, has written some songs[10]). The wheels appeared to be coming off the bus,[11] but he's got so much money, he survived financially — eventually reclaiming his No. 1 spot, although none of it looks like much fun.

And remember, you don't have nearly as much money as Musk to pad the landing when you take a fall.

Frankly, our society loses far too many amazing, much-loved people because they are unfulfilled and unhappy. We ached when icons like Robin Williams, Kurt Cobain, Anthony Bourdain, Kate Spade, and Naomi Judd died by suicide. We wonder if they knew how they had touched the lives of millions of people that they'd never even met. Clearly success and money alone do not guarantee happiness.

My hope is that even one person reads this and makes a much-needed change.

While it is certainly my goal to support your financial well-being, knowing the relationship between money and happiness should be equally significant. It's never too late to turn your life around. Get honest with yourself and reach out to a loved one or a professional to figure out the source of why you might feel unfulfilled, even if you're rich.

Every journey has a starting point. I'd be happy to take your call. I have no doubts we can learn from each other's experiences.

DON'T BE THAT GUY, BE THAT OTHER GUY

On the other hand, there are plenty of examples of people who have built great wealth, or come into sudden wealth, who have not let it go to their head or sour their soul. A couple have already been mentioned.

When I started this project, I felt as if the characteristics of the rich and poor were well-defined in my mind. After all, I've been an investment adviser for more than 15 years and I've seen a wide range of human characteristics.

I can tell you this much: Happy people share one major trait.

Back in 2009, someone I knew invited me to an event his company was sponsoring. The idea was that startups would present their pitches. I was really excited to attend. When I got there, I was overwhelmed by the presenters.

My friend was incredibly well-versed in this particular realm. Yet, after the event, he asked me how the program could have been improved. This took me by surprise as it wasn't my area of expertise; I really knew nothing about it.

Frankly, I didn't feel all that comfortable telling him how things should work in his area of expertise.

But his response really stuck with me. He said he wanted to know what I thought for exactly that reason. I was an outsider, and he needed to know if he had any blind spots. He didn't want to lecture me; he wanted to listen to me.

Here was a leader in his field asking a novice for input about an event his organization hosted.

If you haven't already guessed, a characteristic shared among highly successful people is humility.

Instead of letting their successes go to their heads, they recognize that the ability to constantly improve, check for blind spots, and increase their knowledge base are the keys to remaining successful. And that luck, both good and bad, is always at play.

They know the importance of focusing on today, rather than relishing in yesterday. The moment they become arrogant and feel like they know everything is the moment things begin to falter.

As the great investor George Soros wrote:

> The only thing that could hurt me is if my success encouraged me to return to my childhood fantasies of omnipotence — but that is not likely to happen as long as I remain engaged in the financial markets, because they constantly remind me of my limitations. [12]

Clearly, there is more to being successful than just this one trait. However, it all starts with the ability to recognize what you don't know, rather than advertising what you do. The happiest people I know are always challenging themselves to do better and constantly seeing new ways to better serve their families, customers, and employees. And this makes them better with their money.

It's all actually very simple.

When the focus is on others, great things happen.

How do you recognize these people from the miserable millionaires? Well, if you meet them, you're in awe of how approachable they are.

They will spend more time asking questions about you than talking about themselves. They are focused on the greater good of the team, not the good of the individual (themselves).

As Indra Nooyi, the former CEO of PepsiCo (among other things) put it:

> When you assume negative intent, you're angry. If you take away that anger and assume positive intent, you will be amazed. Your emotional quotient goes up because you are no longer almost random in your response.[13]

Getting right in your soul, which will get you right in your head, will not only lead to better decision-making but better life outcomes.

LESSONS AT A GLANCE

- Do you live in a constant state of discontent?
- Do you seek career success/status over relationships?
- Do you tend to be a workaholic?
- Do you have a clear vision to serve others?
- Do you chase money or continual improvement?
- Do you take responsibility when there's a problem?
- Do you realize that the team is more important than the individual?
- Do you measure success by money or the impact you have on your community?

CHAPTER 10
CHOOSE HOW TO BE RICH

"The biggest reward is not financial benefits, though it's really good, you can get a lot of great shoes! Those of you who have a lot of shoes know having a closet full of shoes doesn't fill up your life. Living a life of substance can."

– Oprah Winfrey

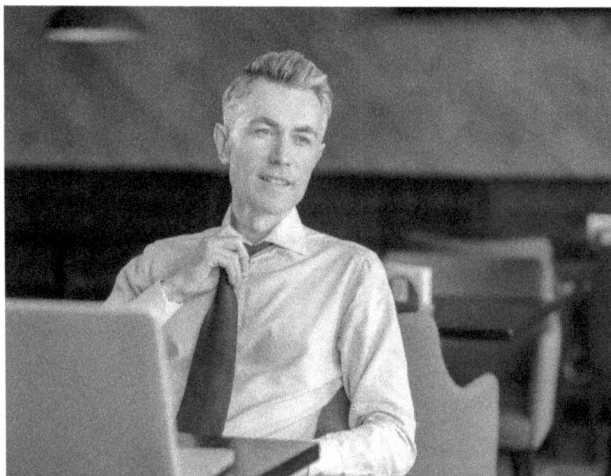

THE BIG RISK   149

Taking your money seriously is important. There's nothing wrong with building, and protecting, your sudden wealth. But that's not a life.

Having a lot of money is nice. It provides peace of mind, security, and comfort. It also affords you the opportunity to be generous — not just with your money but also with your time. After experiencing a windfall of money, being thoughtful in how it's managed is key and so is giving mind to how you're showing up in life despite your drastic increase in wealth.

THE OPEN MILLIONAIRE

I've interviewed so many amazing people who were open with their time and insight.

But one interview in particular had a significant impact on me.

The things we discussed and the lessons I learned have remained at the forefront of my mind as I've written this book. He was gracious enough to sit down with me and be very candid about his world.

I'm a firm believer in spiritual laws, meditation, and how these factors and influences play a role in our lives. I'd wanted to meet this person (we'll call him John) for many years. One of my best friends had worked for him for three decades and told me he'd introduce us at some point, but it never seemed to work out with our schedules.

Unfortunately, my friend was diagnosed with an incurable disease, which eventually ran its course. The funeral service was packed. As guests began to filter in, it became clear there were not enough chairs to seat everyone. Being Jewish, his funeral occurred within 24 hours of his death, so the fact that there were so many people there was a true testament to the impact he had upon the world.

Considering the funeral's short notice and John's intense travel demands, no one expected him to be able to attend the service.

However, sitting in the back of the room marveling at all the people who cared so deeply for my friend, I saw John walk in. He immediately sought out the deceased's wife and son to offer his condolences.

Looking around, I realized that the only open seats were directly behind me. I turned to my fiancé and said, "He's going to sit behind us."

My friend always promised he would introduce me to his boss and today, the day of his funeral, was the day. Even in death, he was still living up to his word. Sure enough, John came over to the empty chairs and sat down.

I realized this was an opportunity that wouldn't come again. But what was I going to say? Was it even possible to *not* make this situation awkward?

I almost didn't turn around, feeling somewhat uncomfortable and assuming he wouldn't want anything to do with me. But remembering my friend's promise, I brushed the negative thoughts aside and introduced myself to him and the gentleman with him.

I told him how our friend had prided himself on being one of the only people inside his organization that had the guts to tell John the truth. He laughed for a moment and told me that was true. Then he said he wished he would've spent more time with him, and that he'd never dealt with death well.

It didn't hit me until a few hours later what an amazing man I'd been talking with.

As successful as he was, he had the humility and honesty to tell me exactly what he was feeling in the moment. He wasn't guarded. He wasn't arrogant or egotistical. He was authentic with me, a complete stranger.

We parted ways after the service. A few days later, I mailed him a handwritten note thanking him for talking with me and asking if we could meet again at some point. I reached out again in mid-December with no response. Then, after the holidays, his administrative assistant got in touch and said he'd like to sit down later in the month.

As my appointment approached, I was incredibly nervous about meeting this industry icon. On the day of our meeting, I wore my typical charcoal suit, white shirt, and blue tie.

My expectation was that he would be dressed in business casual attire at best, but out of pure respect, I felt a suit and tie were appropriate. It didn't bother me that being overdressed would probably make me appear overeager. I was about to take a meeting with a legend and wanted to show the utmost respect.

At his office, I was shown into a conference room and only waited about five to 10 minutes. John entered through the side door with one of his key employees (who I'd met with several times in the past). They both joked, in a good-natured way, at my attire and how formal I looked. It made me laugh, which broke the tension and immediately put me at ease.

One of the things that impressed me so much during our first conversation at the funeral was how John had used humor throughout our time talking. And here we were inside his corporate conference room and it was exactly the same.

As we sat down, the first thing I noticed was how relaxed he was.

It seemed as if he was letting me know I could ask him any question and that he'd stay as long as I wanted him to. Ironically, this relaxed tone made me somewhat uncomfortable. Without a provided time limit, how much of his time should I take? Was 15 minutes appropriate? What about 20? Was 30 minutes pushing it?

When all was said and done, we spent two hours talking. I took the initiative to end the meeting because I was sure he must have something more important to do and that I was wearing out my welcome.

Of course, this wasn't based on anything he did or said. He was completely relaxed and open the entire time, never checking his watch or phone. Nor did his assistant quietly knock on the door to tell him he had another appointment. My feelings were completely based on my own interpretation of what his busy days must be like. And my belief is that, if I hadn't said anything, he would've spent another hour with me.

Of all the things I learned that day, the one that stuck with me the most — the thing that had the most lasting impact — was that his entire life centers around creating meaningful relationships with people.

He is focused on the impact he has on the people around him (as well as the world) and his ability to help people grow and develop both personally and professionally. In fact, he told me that this was his greatest passion. I was fortunate enough to experience it first-hand.

Our range of topics spanned just about everything, from family to business to recreation to our biggest failures. It didn't seem like any topic was off the table.

In all the people I've met professionally, it's rare that I've found someone as candid, honest, and open as John.

He shared success stories he was proud of, failures he learned from, and frustrations he still experienced. Much of what I told him regarded the catalyst for this book: the failure of my firm.

I didn't know if he would be aware of my previous legal issues, but he looked at me and said, "All of us fail. Every single one of us. Some of our failures are bigger than others. It's what you do with the lessons that you've learned."

Part of me was embarrassed to discuss my SEC experience, but it felt important to bring it up.

So, there I was, sitting with one of the wealthiest men in the country and he's telling me it's OK learn from the experience and move on.

"You'll be better for it," he said.

One particularly interesting moment happened at the beginning of the interview when I told him he was probably the wealthiest person nobody's ever heard of. He said he knew that.

It was completely by design; he consciously keeps a low profile.

He's rarely in the paper, even though he gives a significant amount of money to the charitable organizations he holds near and dear to his heart. And he is not generally seen at high-profile events.

He chooses not be in the spotlight because he'd rather give credit to others — specifically, to the people that work for him. They had been so instrumental in helping him build his brand and becoming such a successful businessman.

As we kept talking, I realized that his business philosophy is fascinatingly different from the way most people operate. More questions about that followed.

For example, I noticed when entering his corporate headquarters that there was no display celebrating current accomplishments of the company, whereas most businesses display plaques, certifications, and awards on the walls.

In this case, all of his personal awards, and the business' awards, were in the basement.

Yep. The basement.

His employees worked on the second floor. Why would you put the reminders of the great things you've accomplished in a place where your employees (and clients, for that matter) rarely go? I asked him about this rather unusual arrangement and, again, got a response that surprised me:

"That's what we did yesterday. On the second floor is what we're doing today."

He didn't want to keep yesterday's successes in front of his current employees' faces, or even want them clinging to the things they'd already achieved.

His belief was that the potential for new achievements is what motivates people to wake up every day with a fresh attitude. Today is a new day with new challenges. He doesn't want anyone, including himself, resting on their laurels.

"I don't want to use the successes of my past to dictate my future."

John believes history (both personal and business) is important; however, it has little to no effect on what his business is doing today.

He is a big believer in systems and processes, but places his deepest faith in the people who work for him. He said that, if you have the right people in the right positions and you compensate them in the right way, amazing things happen. The goals you want to reach suddenly don't seem so lofty. The numbers go in the right direction. You don't seem to experience as many problems along the way.

What he's talking about is creating community.

THE GIVING PLEDGE

We need to look out for one another. We can all do something.

The truly wealthy understand that sharing their good fortune is one of the most important things they can do.

Life is not about what you get, but about what you give. This process is how we find happiness.

The Giving Pledge was founded in 2010 by Bill Gates, Melinda French Gates, and Warren Buffett. It is an effort to convince billionaires to "publicly dedicate the majority of their wealth to philanthropy."[1] The essence of this movement is focused on stepping outside of our own lives and helping others.

One person that's embraced this is MacKenzie Scott, the successful novelist who won the American Book Award in 2005 and whose teacher at Princeton — none other than Nobel Prize in Literature winner Toni Morrison — described her as "one of the best students I've ever had in my creative-writing classes … really one of the best."[2]

Oh yeah, she used to be married to Jeff Bezos too.

Her divorce from Amazon's founder made her one of the wealthiest women in the world (talk about sudden wealth!). She promptly went about giving much of her fortune away:

> The miracle, of course, is that Scott — whose divorce from Jeff Bezos happened in a spectacularly public fashion thanks to the *National Enquirer* breaking Bezos's long-term affair publicly — did not get her down. She got even. And not, to public knowledge, by spending her Amazon money all on herself (even though that would be tight). She got even by doing what he does not: sharing his unbelievable, unconscionable, indescribable wealth with those

he makes his money off of, i.e. everyone else in the world. It gives a whole new meaning to "fuck-you money."[3]

She's turned the world of philanthropy on its head, embracing the Giving Pledge to its fullest. In a post on Medium in 2020 — in which she cited Emily Dickenson and a Chicago teenager who had setup a neighborhood support system for people whose work was disrupted by the COVID-19 lockdown — she explained her strategy of giving:

> We do this research and deeper diligence not only to identify organizations with high potential for impact, but also to pave the way for unsolicited and unexpected gifts given with full trust and no strings attached. Because our research is data-driven and rigorous, our giving process can be human and soft. Not only are nonprofits chronically underfunded, they are also chronically diverted from their work by fundraising, and by burdensome reporting requirements that donors often place on them.[4]

Since taking the plunge, Scott has dropped no-strings-attached donations to an incredibly wide array of organizations, from endowment-deprived historically Black colleges and universities (HBCUs) to local food banks to LGBTQ-support groups. With a small team of advisers, she leads an a philanthropic organization, which she founded, called Yield Giving[5] that:

> ... typically informs nonprofits of the largest donations they have ever received through a cold call or following a nondescript email. Her gifts come with no conditions and very few reporting requirements.[6]

But should this kind of giving be carried out by just a few billionaires? Skeptics may say that billionaires can afford to give away half their income, but the rest of us can't.

However, the reality is that nearly all of us can make charitable giving part of our financial plan. I'd argue that we can't afford not to.

We're all in this together. Just as Scott was inspired in part by a teenager who raised $7,000 to support her neighbors,[7] she argues that we all have to pay it forward. When introducing a list of organizations that received her 2020 tranche of giving, she wrote:

> The organizations named below offer a daily reminder that we can each carry more than we imagine. And they offer an opportunity to invest our good fortune in change, no matter what form our good fortune has taken.[8]

Selfless giving can be a challenge for some. What's in it for them is the question they can't escape.

Here's an example. A friend of mine was having an argument with his ex-wife because she decided she wouldn't cover any portion of their child's college tuition (their daughter was over the age of 18 when they divorced so college costs were not covered in the divorce agreement). This situation left my friend feeling very frustrated and angry. He believed it was a joint responsibility. Here's where a less formal type of giving pledge comes in.

I told him it was a selfless act to cover 100% of his kid's college tuition. He would get the opportunity to do an incredible service out of love for his daughter, and despite the losing argument with his ex-wife, he'd actually be winning because his daughter could graduate from college without student loans. What better way to spend his money than on service to his daughter? It was an opportunity his ex would miss out on by refusing to contribute.

My point is that the more we can focus on others, the happier we are.

Focusing on what we don't have and circumstances that we can't control is a fruitless endeavor. The more we follow this line of thinking, the less happy we feel. It's a cycle that continues relentlessly.

As Scott wrote, we can "invest our good fortune ... no matter what form our good fortune has taken." Most people reading this book have probably had some good fortune come their way.

So, although the Giving Pledge asks billionaires to give at least half their money away, I believe it includes all of us.

In the words of the civil rights activist Cesar Chavez:

> We cannot seek achievement for ourselves and forget about progress and prosperity for our community ... Our ambitions must be broad enough to include the aspirations and needs of others, for their sakes and for our own.[9]

Rather than only focusing on your money and what it can do for you, focus instead on a mission of service and gratitude. Making the world a better place is just the right thing to do. Without realizing this, I would never have written this book. It is one of the ways I seek to fulfill my own commitment to the Giving Pledge.

LESSONS AT A GLANCE

- How much money you have measures how well you're playing the money game, not the life game.
- Help people get rich in ways far more valuable than money.
- Take what you need, give what you can.
- Invest your good fortune.

CHAPTER 11
THE $10,000,000
DUMB TAX

"Once I stopped focusing on [money], I became a little bit more successful."

– Shaquille O'Neal

Ten million dollars. Yes, that's what my mistake cost me.

Ten million dollars … and a whole lot more. From what I've shared before, you can see that, given a different attitude and way of doing things, it was all avoidable.

What's scary is that I just didn't see it coming. And if I didn't see it coming, the same thing can probably happen to you and your money.

You might be thinking, "No way! Only stupid people would make such a costly mistake!"

If this is your attitude, be careful. Arrogance got the better of me, and I know I'm not the only one (think back to Elon Musk's massive loss — many report it's around $200 billion[1]).

I had no idea the role behavior played in shaping my reaction to situations. We all operate with coding that is constantly at work in our subconscious mind.

If you doubt this, just go back and analyze any situation and how you reacted. What you will discover is that there is a very predictable pattern that emerges. You may get angry. You may withdraw. You may feel shame. Whatever it is, its activation is pretty automatic. Knowing this information about yourself can be the make or break in safeguarding your sudden wealth. How will you handle all the decisions you need to make to grow your money while keeping it safe?

Behavior patterns are like computer codes. They are the operating system that runs you. But here's what's scary: Once this code is installed, there are no updates, unless you have some sort of epiphany.

And for many of us, epiphanies come the hard way. Having them without the heartache, not to mention the monetary loss, is preferable.

A game-changer for me was the decision to get an outside perspective on myself. There are various ways you can do this such as personal development classes, coaching, or therapy (I did coaching). But the decision to explore oneself is an important step. A mentally healthier you is a better decision-making you.

Exploring my past revealed my blind spots. I discovered a pattern of emotional reactions, and subsequent behavior, that were rooted in my past.

I grew up in an environment of competition. Winning was paramount. It started in my youth, when I competed in water-skiing. Think of competitive water-skiing like America's Cup, where sailing yachts have to navigate a course while being timed, but on water skis.

What I learned as a child was that winning got me rewards and losing got me nothing. I began to build my self-esteem not on who I was, but on what I accomplished. This fueled my need to succeed.

One sunny day in San Diego, when I was only 10 years old, I was competing in the youth division of the National Speed Skiing Championship. Based on my past successes, my family and I weren't surprised when I won the first day of the two-day event.

However, the second day began with success slipping through my fingers — literally. At the start of the race, the handles fell out of my hands and I didn't make it out of the water. The boat had to circle back around to do a restart.

In a two-lap race, that was the end of that. Even though I had won the first-day event, missing the start of the second-day event should have been fatal to my overall chances.

Well … maybe. The boat came back around quickly, and I got up a second time. The next two laps were the fastest I had ever skied. It was a blur. I passed skier after skier. In only two laps, I managed to pass nine skiers to finish third. Based on the two-day total of points, I won the overall event.

And what happened next shaped the rest of my life.

Water-ski racing is a niche sport, but it has a devoted following. National events bring people from all over. After I returned to shore, a roar welcomed me. As I walked around the beach, I was treated like a celebrity. It was weird and cool all at the same time. All the adults seemed to know me, and all the kids wanted to play with me. It felt good.

Have you ever had things fall into place and suddenly feel like a rock star?

Yea, well, the spotlight always gets switched off eventually. Three years later, I wasn't winning races anymore. As a matter of fact, I wasn't even making the medal stand a lot of the time.

My formative years in this hard-driving environment really shaped my future and many of my decision-making behaviors.

As I grew older and my competitive success stalled, people treated me differently. The rock star status from that day on the beach waned. I quickly concluded that winning brought me acceptance and popularity while losing brought me emptiness.

So, subconsciously I made a mental note to pursue success — no matter the context — to gain the external approval I craved. And risk-taking is definitely part of winning water-ski races.

Later in life, winning took the form of having the biggest house, the fastest car, and the newest gadgets. My unquenchable thirst to be the "rock star" of my life left me with no margin for error.

I felt that buying things proved I was winning. I was living the life of that bumper sticker from the 1980s: "He who dies with the most toys wins."

But financially I was strapped, even though I had every opportunity to be saving money. Ironically, the more money I had, the more money I spent, and hence, the more money I needed.

My educational and professional background led me to believe I was immune to making a big, whopping mistake. I had attended The Wharton School to become a Certified Investment Management Analyst (CIMA). I was also an Accredited Investment Fiduciary Auditor (AIFA). I had taught investment management at universities for over 10 years.

And yet, I ended up paying an eight-figure "dumb tax!" How?

Needless to say, reading a book like this one would have greatly changed my life — if I'd paid attention, which I may not have.

I have gone back and deeply analyzed not only my situation but those of others that have taken a ride on the escalator going down. For some, the dumb tax was much smaller, and for others, much bigger.

What are the common themes that tend to play out? What can we learn?

Avoiding mistakes is so much more important than getting a quick, big return.

Sadly, many people think the opposite. They swing for the fences and, in doing so, create their own failure.

The lessons I now teach are all about managing mistakes (i.e., how to avoid making financial blunders that result in paying the dumb tax).

THE SEVEN SINS OF WEALTH MANAGEMENT

I'd like to lay out the seven important takeaways from this book:

Power of Behavior

If you don't handle your emotions, the dumb tax will come due. Emotions drive so many things. Fear, for example, can cause us to make choices we would not normally consider. What is happening in your background operating system? Understand your past to see what is guiding your current decision-making.

Murky Goals

It's not a goal if it's unclear or vague. Ambiguity leads to impulsive actions that sound good in the moment but are doomed because they are not rational. Ideas need to be disciplined by clear, rational guidelines. Always have guardrails.

The Uneducated Investor

How many times have you, or someone you know, purchased something because it sounds so good, only to later learn things that would have completely altered the original decision?

This can even happen when buying a stereo or car. When investing real money, it's best to get educated in a meaningful way. (FYI, this will not happen while looking at a smartphone. Remember, don't be like Gisele and Tom in that Super Bowl crypto ad.)

Trust and Reliance on Others

I see this a lot with wealth creators. They make their money because they are really good at their craft. Perhaps they are artists, inventors, or athletes.

But then they ignore the need to educate themselves about investments because they have no interest in the field. Instead, they defer blindly to others. Yet, such reliance is a dumb tax waiting to happen.

You don't need to become a financial expert, but you do need to develop basic financial understanding regarding how investments work.

Busyness is Not Good for Business

If you find yourself just "too busy" to learn, then the dumb tax will come knocking. You'll be so busy that money will fly out the door. What are you so busy doing? Making money? Ironically, if you slow down long enough to learn a little, you'll make — and keep — more money.

A Fee System That is Not Uniform

The odds are stacked against you. People will sell you products that have the highest commission fees; they won't easily offer the cheapest solution. You can end up with something a salesperson wanted to sell, rather than something you actually want.

Complexity of Investments

If you don't understand it, don't do it. Period. How many crypto investors can explain the core components of a blockchain and how crypto utilizes them to provide meaningful solutions to consumers? Not many, if any.

NEVER MAKE THE ASSUMPTION YOU KNOW ENOUGH

The dumb tax can always be traced back to these seven sins of wealth management. Always. Avoiding them will save you a lot of heartache (and money).

As fast as your sudden wealth appeared, it can vanish equally as fast. Recognize this fact and you will be much more likely to keep it.

Education and personal empowerment are a journey. They are a continual process. Emulate the people who never stop learning no matter how successful they already are:

> Jeff Green, now playing for the Nuggets in his 15th season, learned how to prepare by just watching [LeBron] James's routine. "I always think of him like a high school kid or a college kid, wanting to learn as much as possible, but he's doing it 20 years in, and that's what makes him so great," Green says. "He's never ashamed to ask questions or to reveal that he's still learning this game."[2]

Be committed to understanding your financial life. Never stop learning and examining while also keeping it simple. Say yes to those things that are part of your plan and that you understand. Say NO to everything else.

There is a wealth of information to support you in this process. You can continue your education at my website (www.moneymastery. courses) where you'll find many tools and educational programs to help you on your path. Without such support, protecting your financial future can be challenging. I hope you'll drop me a line to let me know how the journey is going, and reach out to me with any questions or concerns.

Remember, failure is feedback. The key is to learn from others' mistakes (like mine) and avoid making your own. In this way, I can be a partner in your success.

LESSONS AT A GLANCE

- Yes, you can be that stupid.

- Know your coding, i.e., your behavior patterns and motivations.
- Get help if you need it.
- The way to avoid paying the dumb tax is by not doing dumb stuff.

AFTERWORD

Though this book has primarily centered on sudden wealth, it has also explored ways to think about life and the role money plays in it.

To end things, I'd like to share a deeply emotional experience that happened a few years after I hit proverbial rock bottom by running my business, and much else, into the ground.

MY HOLY SH#T MOMENT

My journey back from financial ruin pressured me into learning new ways to view not just money, but life. Since my fall from grace, I've found greater levels of happiness and personal fulfillment that have nothing to do with money.

(Though I will note, as I hope I've shown, that caring a little less about money actually makes it more likely that you'll keep yours!).

Since losing my business, a great influence on my life has been participating in Ironman competitions. Widely considered to be among the most physically challenging endurance contests, in a single day you complete a 2.4-mile swim, a 112-mile bike ride, and a 26.2-mile run. I completed my first Ironman in Arizona in 2017.

But my most profound Ironman experience was when I teamed up with a young man with cerebral palsy, Patrick Utitus-Canez. Although he could not walk, he had completed over 30 marathons and had always wanted to be an Ironman.

For an athlete like Patrick to compete in an Ironman, someone would have to tow him in a raft during the swim, push or pull him with the bike during cycling, and push him in a jogger for the run. I was honored when the founder of 2Gether We Live, an organization that seeks to make a positive difference for those with disabilities or illness, asked me to help Patrick achieve his goal.

This involved not just grueling training for about a year but also bankrolling and designing a new bike that would allow Patrick to ride in the front (rather than being pulled behind it). I threw myself into a fundraising campaign and, unlike things I had wanted in my past, this was not about how money could buy me something new to feed my desires. Instead, it was about helping someone else achieve more in life — about the impact that my money could make.

The race itself was a revelatory experience. I barely made it through the whole thing, but the feeling of accomplishment on the other side was unlike anything I'd ever experienced. When Patrick and I reached the beach after the swim portion, there were cheers. The crowds went absolutely nuts. I was overwhelmed.

We had the honor of inspiring many strangers, a feeling that still lifts my heart years later. This experience brought me a deep sense of personal fulfillment that I'd never felt before. All the endorphin rushes I experienced during my past business wheeling and dealing didn't even come close.

If there's a lesson I hope you can take from this book, it's that ultimately peak personal happiness has nothing to do with money.

Throughout my life, I pursued what others told me was important: money, status, and prestige. While I studiously accumulated more *things*, none of them ever brought me peace.

I guess you could divide my life into two sections:

- The time I spent chasing money.
- The time I spent chasing impact.

Looking back, I realized that before my Ironman experience with Patrick, everything was about me and what I got or didn't get. I was an army of one. The experience with Patrick gave me a different perspective: the power of *we*. As a result, I developed more personal friendships and connections than any business deal ever brought me, ultimately fueling my ability, and my desire, to make an impact.

WEALTH AS A TOOL

By now you know that when you come into sudden wealth, it's not just about the money. It never is.

With wealth in general, and especially the kind that is sudden, you're faced with risks, decisions, and opportunities for not only expanding your wealth but also for your own personal growth. When you have money in the bank, you have the ability to think bigger and use your wealth as a tool to create more impact.

My story is a good reminder to not constantly pursue what's in it for you. After all, this book was inspired by the hard lessons I learned when my pursuit of financial success went way off course. As you've read about in these pages, chasing money and ignoring risk brings down many intelligent people.

The key is for your sudden wealth to be a vehicle that gets you further in life. Don't let it be a vehicle that drives you into a financial ditch. My hope is that this book provides an easy education of developing risk awareness, so you never have to learn the hard way.

———

Connect with Walter:
e: walter@familycfo.net
w: www.familycfo.net

BIBLIOGRAPHY

1. THE CONNECTION BETWEEN EXCESSIVE OPTIMISM AND UNEXPECTED RISK

1. Securities and Exchange Commission [findings and sanctions], *In the Matter of Oxford Investment Partners, LLC, and Walter J. Clarke*, February 15, 2013, https://www.sec.gov/litigation/admin/2013/ia-3554.pdf.
2. Caitlin Moscatello, "The Fleishman Effect: In a City of Rachels and Libbys, the FX Show Has Some New York Moms Worried They're the Ones in Trouble," *The Cut*, February 6, 2023, https://www.thecut.com/2023/02/the-fleishman-is-in-trouble-effect.html.

2. THE EFFECT OF SUDDEN WEALTH

1. "LeBron James Talks About Being a First-Generation Money Maker and Betting on Himself," Chase, n.d., https://www.chase.com/personal/chase-stories/community-leaders/kd-lebron-james.
2. The Notorious B.I.G., "Mo Money Mo Problems (Official Music Video)," YouTube Video, September 6, 2011, https://www.youtube.com/watch?v=gUhRKVIjJtw.
3. Melissa Chan, "Here's How Winning the Lottery Makes You Miserable," *Time*, January 12, 2016, http://time.com/4176128/powerball-jackpot-lottery-winners.
4. Nicole, Bitette, "Curse of the Lottery: Tragic Stories of Big Jackpot Winners," *New York Daily News*, January 12, 2016, http://www.nydailynews.com/lifestyle/tragic-stories-lottery-winners-article-1.2492941.
5. Scott Hankins, Mark Hoekstra, and Paige Marta Skiba. "The Ticket to Easy Street? The Financial Consequences of Winning the Lottery," *3rd Annual Conference on Empirical Legal Studies Papers* (March 26, 2010), https://papers.ssrn.com/sol3/papers.cfm?abstract_id=1134067.
6. Joe McGauley, "Everything MC Hammer Blew His Fortune On," *Thrillist*, March 30, 2014, https://www.thrillist.com/home/why-mc-hammer-went-broke-how-mc-hammer-spent-all-of-his-money.
7. Robert Draper, "Poor Willie," *Texas Monthly*, May 1991, https://www.texasmonthly.com/arts-entertainment/poor-willie.
8. Matthew Perpetua, "Nas Owes the IRS Nearly $6.5 Million," *Rolling Stone*, January 26, 2011, https://www.rollingstone.com/music/music-news/nas-owes-the-irs-nearly-6-5-million-248546.

9. Associated Press, "Lauryn Hill Starts Prison Sentence for Failing to Pay Taxes," *Today*, July 8, 2013, http://www.today.com/entertainment/lauryn-hill-starts-prison-sentence-failing-pay-taxes-6C10570914.

10. Associated Press, "Jermaine Dupri's Atlanta Mansion in Foreclosure,"*Billboard*, December 11, 2014, http://www.billboard.com/articles/columns/the-juice/6405606/jermaine-dupri-atlanta-mansion-foreclosure.

11. Associated Press, "Lawsuit: Depp $2 Million Monthly Spending to Blame for Money Woes," CNBC, January 31, 2017, https://www.cnbc.com/2017/01/31/johnny-depp-star-of-the-pirates-of-the-caribbean-franchise-spent-2-million-each-month-lawsuit-shows.html.

12. Nardine Saad, "'Partridge Family's' David Cassidy Files for Bankruptcy after Divorce, Rehab," *Los Angeles Times*, February 12, 2015, https://www.latimes.com/entertainment/gossip/la-et-mg-david-cassidy-bankruptcy-chapter-11-divorce-20150212-story.html.

13. Bob Allen, "Paul McCartney's One on One Tour Earns $132 Million in 2017," *Billboard*, December 27, 2017, https://www.billboard.com/articles/columns/chart-beat/8085450/paul-mccartney-one-on-one-tour-earnings.

14. Rania Aniftos, "A Timeline of Dolly Parton's Good Deeds," *Billboard*, August 3, 2022, https://www.billboard.com/music/music-news/dolly-parton-good-deeds-timeline-9487782.

15. Joe Hernandez, "Dolly Invested Royalties from Whitney's 'I Will Always Love You' in a Black Community," NPR, August 2, 2021, "https://www.npr.org/2021/08/02/1023889920/dolly-parton-invested-royalties-from-a-whitney-hous ton-cover-in-a-black-communit.

16. Madeline Berg, "Dolly Parton's Net Worth Revealed: The Staggering Success Of America's Country Music Queen," *Forbes*, August 5, 2021, https://www.forbes.com/sites/maddieberg/2021/08/05/dolly-partons-net-worth-revealed-the-staggering-success-of-americas-country-music-queen.

3. KEEPING WEALTH IS HARDER THAN EARNING IT

1. Clay Cockrell, "I'm a Therapist to the Super-Rich: They Are as Miserable as Succession Makes Out," *Guardian*, November 22, 2021, https://www.theguardian.com/commentisfree/2021/nov/22/therapist-super-rich-succes sion-billionaires.

2. Megan Sauer, "Dolly Parton Credits Her Long-Term Success to this 6-Word Piece of Advice from Her Mother," CNBC Make It, March 9, 2022, https://www.cnbc.com/2022/03/09/dolly-parton-my-mothers-advice-led-to-my-finan cial-personal-success.html.

3. Jasmine Kim, "NBA Star-Turned-Businessman Shaq Reveals the Worst Invest-ment He Ever Made," CNBC, August 28, 2019, https://www.cnbc.com/2019/08/28/nba-legend-shaq-reveals-the-worst-investment-he-ever-made.html.

4. Alex Henderson, "I Felt Like We Were in 'Goodfellas: Investors Claim Santos Defrauded Them in 'Ponzi Scheme," *Salon*, January 26, 2023, https://www.

salon.com/2023/01/26/i-felt-like-we-were-in-goodfellas-investors-claim-george-santos-defrauded-them-in-ponzi-scheme_partner.

5. Thorstein Veblen, "Conspicuous Consumption," in *The Theory of the Leisure Class: An Economic Study of Institutions* (New York: Macmillan, 1899), ch. 4.

6. Zoë Schiffer, Casey Newton, and Alex Heath, "Tears, Blunders and Chaos: Inside Elon Musk's Twitter," *Guardian*, January 29, 2023, https://www.theguardian.com/technology/2023/jan/29/tears-blunders-and-chaos-inside-elon-musk-twitter.

7. Ken Sweet, "38 Studios: Broke Rhode Island Now Owns a Video Game Company," CNN Money, May 29, 2012, https://money.cnn.com/2012/05/28/technology/38-studios/index.htm.

4. ADVICE FOR ATHLETES: KEEP YOUR WINDFALL

1. University of Colorado at Boulder, "Average Major League Baseball Career 5.6 Years, Says New Study," ScienceDaily, July 11, 2007, https://www.sciencedaily.com/releases/2007/07/070709131254.htm.

2. Pablo S. Torre, "How (and Why) Athletes Go Broke," *Sports Illustrated*, March 23, 2009, https://www.si.com/vault/2009/03/23/105789480/how-and-why-athletes-go-broke.

3. Kyle Carlson, Joshua Kim, Annamaria Lusardi & Colin F. Camerer, "Bankruptcy Rates Among NFL Players With Short-Lived Income Spikes," NBER Working Paper 21085, 2015, http://www.nber.org/papers/w21085.

4. John Keim, "With Average NFL Career 3.3 Years, Players Motivated to Complete MBA Program," ESPN, July 29, 2016, http://www.espn.com/blog/znflnation/post/_/id/207780/current-and-former-nfl-players-in-the-drivers-seat-after-completing-mba-program.

5. William C. Rhoden, "A Basketball Life of Harsh Reality, Starkly Revisited," *New York Times*, May 10, 2014, https://www.nytimes.com/2014/05/11/sports/basketball/a-basketball-life-of-harsh-reality-starkly-revisited.html.

6. Kent Babb, "Allen Iverson's Sad Saga from All-Star NBA Point Guard to Debt-Ridden Divorcee Revealed in New Book 'Not A Game,'" *New York Daily News*, May 24, 2015, http://www.nydailynews.com/sports/basketball/allen-iverson-sad-saga-revealed-new-book-not-game-article-1.2233445.

7. Jean Song, "Allen Iverson Shoots Down Rumors About His Financial Woes," CBS News, May 15, 2015, http://www.cbsnews.com/news/nba-great-allen-iverson-on-financial-troubles-second-chance-new-documentary.

8. Mike Fish, "Dykstra Creditor Seeks Hearing," ESPN, August 7, 2009, http://www.espn.com/mlb/news/story?id=4383818.

9. Associated Press, "Lenny Dykstra Sentenced for Fraud," ESPN, December 3, 2012, http://www.espn.com/mlb/story/_/id/8706890/lenny-dykstra-sentenced-six-months-prison-bankruptcy-fraud-case.

10. Aimee Picchi, "LeBron James Is Officially a Billionaire," CBS News, June 3, 2022, https://www.cbsnews.com/news/lebron-james-billionaire-how-did-lebron-james-become-a-billionaire.

11. "LeBron James Talks About Being a First-Generation Money Maker and Betting on Himself," Chase, n.d., https://www.chase.com/personal/chase-stories/community-leaders/kd-lebron-james.
12. Zameena Mejia, "Warren Buffett Said LeBron James Has a 'Money Mind' — Here's Why," CNBC, October 8, 2018, https://www.cnbc.com/2018/10/08/warren-buffett-said-lebron-james-has-a-money-mind--heres-why.html.
13. Zameena Mejia, "Warren Buffett Said LeBron James Has a 'Money Mind' — Here's Why," CNBC.
14. Kareem Abdul-Jabbar, "Magic Johnson and Money Matters," ESPN, April 10, 2012, http://www.espn.com/espn/commentary/story/_/page/abdul-jabbar-120409/the-magic-johnson-template-pro-athletes-their-money-management.
15. Jennifer Vineyard, "The A-List Accountant Who Tries to Keep Celebrities From Going Broke," New York, April 6, 2017, http://nymag.com/thejob/2017/04/the-accountant-who-tries-to-keep-celebrities-from-going-broke.html.
16. Scott Cohn, "Twenty Years after Epic Bankruptcy, Enron Leaves a Complex Legacy," CNBC, December 2, 2021, https://www.cnbc.com/2021/12/02/twenty-years-after-epic-bankruptcy-enron-leaves-a-complex-legacy.html.

5. AVOID FEAR AND GREED AT ALL COSTS

1. Paul A. Merriman, "The Genius of Warren Buffett in 23 Quotes," MarketWatch, August 19, 2015, http://www.marketwatch.com/story/the-genius-of-warren-buffett-in-23-quotes-2015-08-19.
2. A Tribe Called Quest, "Midnight," YouTube Video, November 7, 2014, https://www.youtube.com/watch?v=Ljie-zx-pXw.
3. Bob Frick, "Janus Rebuilt: With New Leadership and Improved Returns, This One-Time Comet Is on Another Streak," Kiplinger, June 29, 2007, http://www.kiplinger.com/article/investing/t041-c000-s002-janus-rebuilt.html.
4. Bob Frick, "Janus Rebuilt: With New Leadership and Improved Returns, This One-Time Comet Is on Another Streak," Kiplinger.
5. Parikshit Mishra and Sam Reynolds, "Crypto.com Cuts 20% Workforce as Firm Braces for Crypto Winter: The Exchange is the Latest among the Major Crypto Firms to Announce Layoffs," CoinDesk, January 13, 2023, https://www.coindesk.com/business/2023/01/13/cryptocom-cuts-workforce-by-nearly-20.
6. Angela Watercutter, "These Crypto Super Bowl Ads Feel Like Pets.com All Over Again," Wired, February 11, 2022, https://www.wired.com/story/crypto-super-bowl.
7. "Pets.Com: Please Don't Go," AdAge, January 30, 2000, https://adage.com/videos/petscom-please-don't-go/900.
8. Andrew Beattie, "Why Did Pets.com Crash So Drastically?," Investopedia, October 31, 2021, https://www.investopedia.com/ask/answers/08/dotcom-pets-dot-com.asp.
9. Kimberly Amadeo, "Dow Jones Highest Closing Records: The Dow's Top Highs and Lows Since 1929," the balance, December 21, 2022, https://www.thebalance.com/dow-jones-closing-history-top-highs-and-lows-since-1929-3306174.

10. Sue Grafton, *X* (New York: G. P. Putnam's, 2015).

6. HOW TO TURN $100 MILLION INTO NOTHING

1. How Elon Bought Twitter with Other People's Money [audio]," Planet Money, November 30, 2022, https://www.npr.org/transcripts/1139964806.
2. Camila Domonoske, "Tesla's Stock Lost Over $700 Billion in Value: Elon Musk's Twitter Deal Didn't Help," NPR, January 6, 2023, https://www.npr.org/2023/01/06/1146941980/tesla-shares-elon-musk-twitter-electric-cars.
3. "Elon Musk Sells Another $3.6 Billion in Tesla Stock to Prop Up Twitter," *Forbes*, December 29, 2022, https://www.forbes.com/sites/qai/2022/12/29/elon-musk-sells-another-36-billion-in-tesla-stock-to-prop-up-twitter/?sh=420918b36993.
4. Matt Schulz, "2022 Credit Card Debt Statistics," LendingTree, December 13, 2022, https://www.lendingtree.com/credit-cards/credit-card-debt-statistics.
5. "U.S. Trust Survey Finds Modern American Family Dynamics Complicate Wealth Management: New Study Explores Views on Family, Income Equality and Investing Among Wealthy," Business Wire, June 20, 2014, https://www.businesswire.com/news/home/20140620005091/en/U.S.-Trust-Survey-Finds-Modern-American-Family-Dynamics-Complicate-Wealth-Management.
6. Matthew Frankel, "5 Ways Rich People Use Credit," The Motley Fool, June 29, 2014, https://www.fool.com/investing/general/2014/06/29/5-ways-rich-people-use-credit.aspx.
7. Gerri Detweiler, "How Rich People Use Credit Cards Differently from the Rest of Us," *Insider*, February 18, 2015, http://www.businessinsider.com/how-rich-people-use-credit-cards-differently-than-the-rest-of-us-2015-2.

7. PROCESS VS. STRATEGY: HOW NOT TO GET SCREWED

1. Quiver Quantitative, "The Inverse Jim Cramer Strategy," Seeking Alpha, August 11, 2022, https://seekingalpha.com/article/4533169-the-inverse-jim-cramer-strategy.
2. Suraj Srinivasan and Jonah S. Goldberg, "Recovering Trust After Corporate Misconduct at Wells Fargo," Harvard Business School Case Collection, June 2020, https://www.hbs.edu/faculty/Pages/item.aspx?num=58343.
3. Carlos Waters, "Here's What the Wells Fargo Cross-Selling Scandal Means for the Bank's Growth," CNBC, October 19, 2022, https://www.cnbc.com/2022/10/19/heres-what-the-wells-fargo-cross-selling-scandal-means-for-the-bank.html.
4. Emily Glazer, "Whistleblowers Detail Wells Fargo Wealth Management Woes," *The Wall Street Journal*, July 27, 2018, https://www.wsj.com/articles/whistle blowers-detail-wells-fargo-wealth-management-woes-1532707096.
5. Carlos Waters, "Here's What the Wells Fargo Cross-Selling Scandal Means for the Bank's Growth," CNBC.

6. Camila Domonoske, "Tesla's Stock Lost Over $700 Billion In Value: Elon Musk's Twitter Deal Didn't Help," NPR.
7. Richard Mille (eds. Rob LaFranco and Chase Peterson-Withorn), "World's Billionaires List: The Richest in 2023," *Forbes*, accessed June 22, 2023, https://www.forbes.com/billionaires.
8. Emma Roth, "Here's Everything That Went Wrong with FTX," *The Verge*, November 30, 2022, https://www.theverge.com/2022/11/30/23484331/ftx-explained-cryptocurrency-sbf-sam-bankman-fried.
9. Luc Olinga, "FTX Collapse: Tom Brady And Powerful Billionaires Lose Big," The Street, January 10, 2023, https://www.thestreet.com/investors/ftx-collapse-tom-brady-and-powerful-billionaires-lose-big.
10. "Usain Bolt Lawyers Say $12.7m is Missing from Olympic Champion's Account," *Guardian*, January 18, 2023, https://www.theguardian.com/sport/2023/jan/18/usain-bolt-missing-money-investment-account-jamaica.
11. muzzlightyear, "Tom Brady Crypto Commercial for FTX Exchange," YouTube Video, November 21, 2022, https://www.youtube.com/watch?v=_aCGMyrFn-8.
12. Louis Adam, "Samuel Bankman-Fried: The Fallen FTX CEO No Longer Worth $16 Billion," *Le Monde*, November 29, 2022, https://www.lemonde.fr/en/pixels/article/2022/11/29/samuel-bankman-fried-the-fallen-ftx-ceo-no-longer-worth-16-billion_6005980_13.html.

8. MAKING FEWER DECISIONS: THE PASSIVE APPROACH

1. "Quantitative Analysis of Investor Behavior," Dalbar, n.d., http://www.dalbar.com/ProductsAndServices/QAIB.
2. Nicole Friedman, "Only a Market Crash Can Stop Warren Buffett From Winning This $1 Million Bet," *The Wall Street Journal*, February 23, 2017, https://www.wsj.com/articles/only-a-market-crash-can-stop-warren-buffett-from-winning-this-1-million-bet-1487851203.
3. "Berkshire's Performance vs. the S&P 500," Berkshire Hathaway, February 24, 2018, http://www.berkshirehathaway.com/letters/2017ltr.pdf.
4. Murray Coleman, "SPIVA 2022: Year-End Active vs. Passive Scorecard," March 20, 2023, https://www.ifa.com/articles/despite_brief_reprieve_2018_spiva_report_reveals_active_funds_fail_dent_indexing_lead_-_works.
5. Dennis K. Berman and Jamie Heller, "Wall Street's 'Do-Nothing' Investing Revolution," *The Wall Street Journal*, October 17, 2016, http://graphics.wsj.com/passivists.
6. Anne Tergesen and Jason Zweig, "The Dying Business of Picking Stocks," *The Wall Street Journal*, October 17, 2016, https://www.wsj.com/articles/the-dying-business-of-picking-stocks-1476714749.
7. Anne Tergesen and Jason Zweig, "The Dying Business of Picking Stocks," *Wall Street Journal*.
8. Tim Edwards, et al. SPIVA U.S. Scorecard, S&P Dow Jones Indices. Accessed July 5, 2023, https://www.spglobal.com/spdji/en/documents/spiva/spiva-us-

year-end-2022.pdf.

9. John Tierney, "Do You Suffer From Decision Fatigue?" *New York Times*, August 17, 2011, http://www.nytimes.com/2011/08/21/magazine/do-you-suffer-from-decision-fatigue.html.

10. Jim Sollisch, "The Cure for Decision Fatigue," *The Wall Street Journal*, June 10, 2016, https://www.wsj.com/articles/the-cure-for-decision-fatigue-1465596928.

11. Shai Danziger, Jonathan Levav, and Liora Avnaim-Pesso, "Extraneous Factors in Judicial Decisions," *Proceedings of the National Academy of Sciences of the United States of America* 108, no. 17 (2011), http://www.pnas.org/content/108/17/6889.

12. Alex Frew McMillan, "Buffett Hits a Bumpy Road," CNNMoney, January 20, 2000, https://money.cnn.com/2000/01/20/investing/q_buffett.

13. Andrew Bary, "What's Wrong, Warren?" *Barron's*, December 27, 1999, http://www.barrons.com/articles/SB945992010127068546.

14. Michael Melissinos, "Warren Buffett's Worst Loss Came During the Dot-Com Bubble," Melissinos Trading, June 14, 2018, https://www.melissinostrading.com/warren-buffetts-worst-loss-came-during-the-dot-com-bubble.

15. Deborah Gage, "How Do Investors Get Rich? By Finding 'The 'Winning 15,'" *The Wall Street Journal*, April 27, 2012, https://www.wsj.com/articles/BL-DJINB-1001.

16. Paul A. Merriman, "The Genius of Warren Buffett in 23 Quotes," MarketWatch, August 19, 2015, http://www.marketwatch.com/story/the-genius-of-warren-buffett-in-23-quotes-2015-08-19.

17. C. Ellis, *Winning the Loser's Game: Timeless Strategies for Successful Investing*, McGraw-Hill, 2013.

18. Mitch Tuchman, "Warren Buffett to Heirs: Put My Estate in Index Funds," MarketWatch, March 13, 2014, http://www.marketwatch.com/story/warren-buffett-to-heirs-put-my-estate-in-index-funds-2014-03-13.

19. "ICI Research Perspective: Trends in the Expenses and Fees of Funds, 2022," Investment Company Institute, March 2022. https://www.ici.org/system/files/2022-03/per28-02_2.pdf.

20. Timothy W. Martin, "What Does Nevada's $35 Billion Fund Manager Do All Day? Nothing," *The Wall Street Journal*, October 19, 2016, https://www.wsj.com/articles/what-does-nevadas-35-billion-fund-manager-do-all-day-nothing-1476887420.

21. Timothy W. Martin, "What Does Nevada's $35 Billion Fund Manager Do All Day? Nothing," *The Wall Street Journal*.

9. MISERABLE MILLIONAIRE OR ENLIGHTENED BILLIONAIRE

1. itsathwv, "Show Me the Money," YouTube Video, June 9, 2013, https://www.youtube.com/watch?v=FFrag8ll85w.

2. Talking Heads, "Once in a Lifetime (Official Video)," YouTube Video, February 2, 2018, https://www.youtube.com/watch?v=5IsSpAOD6K8.

3. Raquel Maria Dillon, "Tesla CEO Elon Musk Makes Bold Moves in His First Day Leading Twitter," NPR, October 28, 2022, https://www.npr.org/2022/10/28/1132405405/tesla-ceo-elon-musk-makes-bold-moves-in-his-first-day-leading-twitter.

4. Oliver Darcy, "Elon Musk Bans Several Prominent Journalists from Twitter, Calling into Question His Commitment to Free Speech," CNN, December 16, 2022, https://www.cnn.com/2022/12/15/media/twitter-musk-journalists-hnk-intl/index.html.

5. Thomas Barrabi, "Twitter Employees Using Own Toilet Paper After Elon Musk Cuts Janitors," *New York Post*, December 30, 2022, https://nypost.com/2022/12/30/twitter-employees-using-own-toilet-paper-offices-stink-after-musk-cut-janitors-report.

6. Nicolas Vega, "Elon Musk's $182 Billion Net Worth Drop Breaks Guinness World Record," *CNBC Make It*, January 10, 2023, https://www.cnbc.com/2023/01/10/elon-musk-guinness-world-record-biggest-net-worth-drop.html.

7. Kyle Wiggers, "Musk Blames 'Activist Groups' for Major Advertisers Pausing Spending on Twitter," TechCrunch, November 4, 2022, https://techcrunch.com/2022/11/04/musk-blames-activist-groups-for-major-advertisers-pausing-spending-on-twitter.

8. U2, "I Still Haven't Found What I'm Looking For (Official Music Video)," YouTube Video, October 17, 2016, https://www.youtube.com/watch?v=e3-5YC_oHjE.

9. Ella Alexander, "Life Lessons from Dolly Parton: What Would Dolly Do?," *Harper's Bazaar*, January 19, 2021, https://www.harpersbazaar.com/uk/people-parties/people-and-parties/news/a26180/dolly-parton-quotes.

10. Daniela Avila, "Grimes Seemingly Sings About Elon Musk in 'Player of Games': 'He'll Aways Love the Game' More," *People*, December 6, 2021, https://people.com/music/grimes-seemingly-trolls-elon-musk-in-new-single.

11. Tom Maloney and Dana Hull, "Elon Musk Might Never Be the World's Richest Person Again," *Bloomberg*, January 10, 2023, https://www.bloomberg.com/graphics/2023-elon-musk-might-never-be-worlds-richest-person-again.

12. George Soros, *The Alchemy of Finance* (New York: Wiley, 2003), 373.

13. Michael Diamond, "Indra Nooyi: 'Assume Positive Intent,'" March 6, 2019, https://www.michaeldiamond.com/indra-nooyi-assume-positive-intent.

10. CHOOSE HOW TO BE RICH

1. "About the Giving Pledge," The Giving Pledge, n.d., https://givingpledge.org/About.aspx.

2. Rebecca Johnson, "MacKenzie Bezos: Writer, Mother of Four, and High-Profile Wife," *Vogue*, February 20, 2013, https://www.vogue.com/article/a-novel-perspective-mackenzie-bezos.

3. Kenzie Bryant, "MacKenzie Scott Redefines F--ck-You Money," *Vanity Fair*, December 16, 2020, https://www.vanityfair.com/style/2020/12/mackenzie-scott-redefines-fuck-you-money.

4. MacKenzie Scott, "384 Ways to Help," Medium, December 15, 2000, https://mackenzie-scott.medium.com/384-ways-to-help-45d0b9ac6ad8.
5. Yield Giving, n.d., https://yieldgiving.com.
6. Thalia Beaty and the Associated Press, "MacKenzie Scott Reveals Nearly $2 Billion in Donations to 343 Organizations as She Continues Quest to Give Away Wealth," *Fortune*, November 14, 2022, https://fortune.com/2022/11/14/mackenzie-scott-nearly-2-billion-donations-343-organizations-megadonor-philanthropy.
7. MacKenzie Scott, "384 Ways to Help," Medium.
8. MacKenzie Scott, "116 Organizations Driving Change," Medium, July 28, 2020, https://mackenzie-scott.medium.com/116-organizations-driving-change-67354c6d733d.
9. "Who We Are," Cesar Chavez Foundation, n.d., https://chavezfoundation.org/who-we-are.

11. THE $10,000,000 DUMB TAX

1. Nicolas Vega, "Elon Musk's $182 Billion Net Worth Drop Breaks Guinness World Record," *CNBC Make It*.
2. Mirin Fader, "LeBron, Kareem, and the Secrets to Greatness," *The Ringer*, February 7, 2023, https://www.theringer.com/nba/2023/2/7/23587504/lebron-james-scoring-record-kareem-abdul-jabbar.

www.ingramcontent.com/pod-product-compliance
Lightning Source LLC
Chambersburg PA
CBHW080135240326
41458CB00136B/6930/J